ARGONAUTIKA

Argonautika

The Voyage of Jason and the Argonauts

MARY ZIMMERMAN

NORTHWESTERN UNIVERSITY PRESS
EVANSTON, ILLINOIS

Northwestern University Press
www.nupress.northwestern.edu

Argonautika: The Voyage of Jason and the Argonauts was adapted primarily from two versions of the ancient tale: *The Argonautika,* by Apollonios Rhodios, translated by Peter Green; and *The Voyage of the Argo: The Argonautica of Gaius Valerius Flaccus,* translated by David Slavitt.

Photographs copyright © Liz Lauren from the Lookingglass Theatre production.

Printed in the United States of America

1   0   9   8   7   6   5   4   3   2   1

LIBRARY OF CONGRESS CATALOGING-IN-PUBLICATION DATA

Zimmerman, Mary.
  Argonautika : the voyage of Jason and the Argonauts / Mary Zimmerman.
     p. cm.
  "Argonautika: The Voyage of Jason and the Argonauts was adapted primarily from two versions of the ancient tale: The Argonautika, by Apollonios Rhodios, translated by Peter Green; and The Voyage of the Argo: The Argonautica of Gaius Valerius Flaccus, translated by David Slavitt."
  Includes bibliographical references.
  ISBN 978-0-8101-2606-0 (pbk. : alk. paper)
  1. Apollonius, Rhodius—Adaptations. 2. Valerius Flaccus, Gaius, 1st cent.—Adaptations. 3. Argonauts (Greek mythology)—Drama. 4. Jason (Greek mythology)—Drama. 5. Medea (Greek mythology)—Drama. I. Green, Peter, 1924– II. Slavitt, David R., 1935– III. Apollonius, Rhodius. Argonautica. IV. Valerius Flaccus, Gaius, 1st cent. Argonautica. V. Title.
  PS3576.I66A89 2013
  812.54—dc23

                              2012020387

♾ The paper used in this publication meets the minimum requirements of the American National Standard for Information Sciences—Permanence of Paper for Printed Library Materials, ANSI Z39.48-1992.

To the cast and crew of the Argo

CONTENTS

PRODUCTION HISTORY

The world premiere of *Argonautika* took place at the Lookingglass Theatre in Chicago on October 28, 2006, directed by Mary Zimmerman.

Jason and others	Ryan Artzberger
Hera and others	Lisa Tejero
Athena and others	Mariann Mayberry
Pelias and others	Allen Gilmore
Idmon and others	Jesse Perez
Meleager and others	Dan Kenney
Castor and others	Larry DiStasi
Pollux and others	Tony Hernandez
Hercules, Aeëtes, and others	Glenn Fleshler
Hylas and others	Jarrett Sleeper
Andromeda and others	Victoria Caciopoli
Amycus and others	David Catlin
Aphrodite and others	Angela Walsh
Medea and others	Atley Loughridge

Scenic design was by Daniel Ostling; costumes were by Ana Kuzmanic; and lighting design was by John Culbert. Sound design and composition were by Andre Pluess and Ben Sussman. Puppets were designed and built by Michael Montenegro. Jonathan Templeton was the production stage manager. Rachel Kraft was executive director and David Catlin the artistic director at the Lookingglass Theatre.

The production subsequently appeared in the 2007–2008 season at Berkeley Repertory Theatre; at the Shakespeare Theatre in Washington, D.C.; and at the McCarter Theatre in Princeton. Mary Zimmerman directed all of these productions.

A NOTE ON THE PRODUCTION DESIGN

The design for the play should be open, flexible, and in some way evoke a ship. There should be plenty of ways to get on and off rapidly, some "above" area for gods to loiter in, and allowance for different scenes to share the stage simultaneously. Below is a description of the original production design: take it or leave it, as you see fit. Whatever the design, scenes should shift seamlessly, very rapidly, even overlapping each other, and without blackouts; the separation of scenes in the script in no way implies a pause or break in the action. Musical underscoring can help make the transitions and the narration beautiful. Whether underscored or not, narration should rarely stand alone, but be accompanied by some amplifying image or action.

Argonautika was originally staged in an alley configuration with the audience on both sides of the playing area. The set was a long, rectangular, wide-planked wooden box comprised of a floor, a ceiling, and two sidewalls. It was about fourteen feet deep, forty-four feet long, and seventeen feet high. This design was subsequently used on tour in traditional proscenium houses with only minor modifications (including a slight rake of the floor and tilt of the ceiling). The box had no "back wall" in either configuration: in one case it was open to the second half of the audience, and in the other to the distant back wall of the theater.

The box, or ship, was bisected vertically by a thick mast and transected horizontally by a bridge about four feet wide and nine feet above the deck. The bridge could be accessed from below by portable wooden ship's ladders and from above by a drawbridge lowered from one sidewall. In the case of the alley configuration, the main bridge joined with the balcony level of the black box theater on both ends. In the case of the proscenium configuration, it made a turn and continued offstage downstage of the sidewall of the box. The stage-right wall of the box contained a wide door and the drawbridge above; the stage-left wall had two narrower doors and a window above. When all these apertures were closed, the box appeared seamless and solid.

Running the entire interior circumference of the box were two lanes of grating, each about a foot wide, behind which lighting instruments were concealed. The deck had a trapdoor used for the appearance of the Ghost in "Visitation," the stream in "Hercules," Medea's descent into the underworld, and many other things. In the ceiling, directly above the trap in the floor, there was an opening for the occasional appearance of gods, for the manipulation of the baby puppet in "Visitation," and for dropping ropes, shredded gold, and so on. During "Launch" a bit of "ship's rigging" was added to the set, and oarlocks were placed along the edges of the deck both upstage and downstage. During intermission this additional rigging was taken away.

Great use was made of miniature ships; little *Argos* of varying sizes pulled on strings or manipulated by the gods. The Argonauts sometimes carried long oars and sometimes carried poles that could be used as both oars and spears. The ocean and river were strips or blocks of fabric, manipulated by the actors. The Harpies, the baby, and the dragon were all puppets. (The appendix contains additional notes on these and on other specific staging challenges.) Many members of the original company were physically gifted—able to shimmy up ropes, curl down and drop from the bridge to the lower deck without any aid, lift and transport each other, and generally carry on like Argonauts.

ARGONAUTIKA

CHARACTERS

ARGONAUTS

Jason

Pelias's Son

Idmon

Meleager

Castor

Pollux

Tiphys

Hercules

Hylas

Atalanta

Uncle (of Meleager)

Polyphemus

Zetes

Euphemos

GODS AND CREATURES

Hera

Athena

Ghost

Boreas

Rumor

Dryope, a water nymph

Amycus, a monstrous boxer

Aphrodite

Eros

Fury

Goddesses of the Desert

OTHERS

Pelias, King of Iolcos

Cepheus, a servant

Asterion, a servant

Alcimede, Jason's Mother

Aeson, Jason's Father

Andromeda

Four Women of Lemnos

Dymas

Phineus

Aeëtes's Servant

Aeëtes, King of Colchis

Medea, Aeëtes's Daughter

Styrus, Medea's Fiancé

Apsyrtos, Medea's Brother

Colchian Messenger

Meleager's Mother

Additional characters include various servants, bulls, Harpies, sea monsters, skeleton soldiers, and others.

ACT I

INVOCATION

[*The company enters and the actors take up various positions on the stage while the houselights are still up. As they settle, the houselights go down.*]

ALL:
Sing in us, Muse, the story of Jason and his Argonauts,
how he was sent away on the first voyage of the world
to bring back the Golden Fleece, remnant of the flying ram
that carried away the little children Phrixus and Helle
when their father was about to murder them.
The golden ram flew over the ocean no one had ever sailed
to far-off, stony Colchis, all unknown.
And Jason was sent to bring its remnants back.
What was it like when the world was so young?
Let us see the stars in the night sky above our heads,
let us feel the swell of the waves under our feet,
let us hear the snap of the sail in our ears.
Let us and those who hear us be generous.

Let us be good.
Let us please.
Let us.
Please.

THE STORM

[*Thunder.* JASON *is midstream; the black water of the river ripples around him.* HERA, *disguised as an old woman in a shabby raincoat, holding an umbrella, is on the shore behind him.*]

HERA:
Young man?

[JASON *turns back to look.*]

Take pity on a poor old woman; carry me .across the river. If I try myself, I will surely drown. You're fine and strong—will you help me?

JASON:
The gods grant me power, I will.

[*He returns for her.*]

HERA:
Why thank you, thank you, kind sir. Now, how shall we . . . Shall we—?

[*They struggle to get her on his shoulders.*]

Oh. Oh my. Ah, there we are.

JASON:
You are secure, madame?

HERA:
Oh yes. Quite secure.

JASON:
Here we go. Hold fast.

[*They begin to cross.* ATHENA *enters behind them, with her long spear. She follows their slow progress.*]

HERA:
I am so grateful, kind sir. I've never seen the river run so fast. Never in all my days. What is your name that I might remember you and bless you?

JASON:
Jason.

[*Thunder.*]

HERA:
And where are you headed, Jason?

JASON:
To Iolcos.

HERA:
Why are you headed there?

JASON:
It is my uncle's birthday.

HERA:
What a coincidence! It is King Pelias's birthday as well.

JASON:
King Pelias is my uncle.

HERA:
Oh! Why lucky you.

JASON:
Some might say.

HERA:
Some? Not all?

JASON:
Some say it was my father should be king. Some say a great injustice was done when—

[ATHENA *catches the heel of* JASON's *sandal with the tip of her long spear and holds it down in the riverbed.*]

Oh.

HERA:
What's the matter?

JASON:
My sandal is caught in the riverbed.

HERA [*pressing herself down with all her weight*]:
I am too heavy. I have made you sink. Oh dear—

JASON:
No, no, madame—

HERA:
What shall we do—?

JASON [*trying to reach back to the loose sandal*]:
It's just, it's just . . .

HERA:
Why don't you leave it?

JASON:
No, I think I can reach . . . if I just . . .

HERA:
Just leave it.

JASON:
No, I think I can—

HERA [*striking him with her umbrella*]:
Leave it!

JASON:
Perhaps you are right.

[*He pulls his foot from the sandal, and* ATHENA *exits with it hanging from her spear. For the rest of the play* JASON *will wear only one sandal.*]

HERA:
Well.

[*Pause.*]

You were saying . . . about your father?

JASON:
It doesn't bear repeating.

HERA:
Won't you tell me?

JASON:
Some still say my father is the rightful king, unjustly deposed by his own brother, Pelias.

HERA:
Don't despair. You know those gods—they work in strange ways.

JASON:
That's true.

HERA:
One never knows what they're up to or when they might turn up. Oh, here we are. Safe and sound except for your poor sandal.

JASON [*setting her down*]:
Yes, madame. There you go.

HERA:
Thank you, Jason. Here we part ways.

JASON:
Farewell, madame.

HERA:
Only Jason . . . let me tell you one more thing . . .

[*She drops her umbrella and slips out of her raincoat, revealing her splendid goddess self. Her voice changes as well.*]

I will always love you.

[*She rises and begins to fly off in a shower of gold.*]

JASON:
Oh Goddess!

HERA:
Remember me, Jason. In all your troubles Hera is by your side.

[*She exits as* ATHENA *appears behind* JASON.]

ATHENA:
And Athena, your reason, will guide you.

PELIAS WAS OLD

[*Drums. The palace of* KING PELIAS. *Two servants,* CEPHEUS *and* ASTERION, *enter. They are followed by* KING PELIAS—*ancient, with a long white beard to the floor, a cane, and a spiderweb in the crooked thorns of his crown. Somewhere a clock is ticking wearily.*]

CEPHEUS AND ASTERION:
Pelias was old.

PELIAS:
Cepheus!

CEPHEUS:
My gracious king?

PELIAS:
Get me the blue pills and the black powder. And the green ointment and the purple herbs. And bring both the yellow potion and the clear one.

[CEPHEUS *goes.*]

ASTERION:
Are you not well, most noble and fantastic king?

PELIAS:
My back is sore, my eyes itch; I can neither stand up straight nor sit down. I can no longer taste or smell the food I eat, and all of it makes me retch. My skin is a scratchy, moldy hide that drives me mad. My life is a howling misery. And on top of that, I am continually plagued by one great dread.

ASTERION:
What is that, wise and omnipotent leader?

PELIAS:
That I might die.

ASTERION:
The gods forbid it.

PELIAS:

I dreamt again last night of a man with one sandal. You know what that means?

ASTERION:

No, my most handsome and adorable king.

PELIAS:

The prophecy, man! The prophecy! I'll meet my death by the hand of a one-sandaled man.

ASTERION:

It will never happen.

PELIAS:

Of course it won't! You think I can't outwit whoever comes my way? As long as I can see him coming he won't get near. Today is . . . What is it, today? You know—what is it? It's something! Tell me!

ASTERION:

It is your honorable birthday.

PELIAS:

That's it.

ASTERION:

The people are coming from far and wide to celebrate.

PELIAS:

I hate them.

ASTERION:

Rightly so.

[CEPHEUS *reenters with medicines.*]

CEPHEUS:
Gracious and lovely—

PELIAS:
Bring those here. What is it? What's the matter?

CEPHEUS:
You have a visitor.

PELIAS:
Oh? Who is it, man? Speak up.

CEPHEUS:
Your nephew Jason.

PELIAS:
Jason? Jason has come? Is he armed? Alone? Or with a company of men?

CEPHEUS:
He is alone and unarmed. He says he's come to wish you a happy birthday.

PELIAS:
Ha! That may be true, or it may be some trick.

CEPHEUS:
Sire, there's something else . . .

PELIAS:
Well? Don't be mysterious!

CEPHEUS:
He is wearing only one sandal.

[*Loud thunder.*]

ASTERION:
I'll kill him now.

PELIAS:
No, no, man! We can't do that! So this is what the gods do to amuse themselves: my brother's son and the one-sandaled man that has been prophesied are the same!

ASTERION:
Just as I say—we must kill him now.

PELIAS:
No, you fool! There's the wretched people to think of. They have their ideas! They might rise up against me! Some still favor his father . . .

ASTERION:
But you must be rid of him.

PELIAS:
Of course I must, and I will.

CEPHEUS:
Let me ram him through.

PELIAS:

What did you say?

CEPHEUS:

Let me kill him.

PELIAS:

No. What did you say? Exactly. What did you say?

CEPHEUS:

Let?

PELIAS:

No, no . . . go on.

CEPHEUS:

Me?

PELIAS:

Go on . . . go on . . .

CEPHEUS:

Ram?

PELIAS:

That's it. That's it. [*Gleefully*] Oh, I have the answer. I know just what to do. Send him in, send him in.

[CEPHEUS *goes.*]

ASTERION:

May I ask, what has your incomparable mind conceived?

PELIAS:
Never you mind. Watch and learn, young man, watch and learn.

[CEPHEUS *and* JASON *enter.* HERA *enters above and watches.*]

JASON:
Honored uncle. I've come to wish you cheer on this your birthday.

PELIAS [*adopting an enfeebled air*]:
Most welcome, Jason, most welcome. What has it been, sir, twenty years?

[PELIAS *seems almost to have a heart attack and falls into* JASON's *arms.*]

JASON:
Are you ailing, sir?

PELIAS:
My nephew, beloved, you've come just in time, just in time. You see how aged I am, how frail. It is providence you've come: it is a sign, surely.

JASON:
A sign?

PELIAS:
It is time, my nephew, time for your old uncle to surrender the throne. This morning, this birthday of mine, I woke up knowing in my bones that it was so. And suddenly, here you are.

JASON [*stunned*]:
My lord.

PELIAS:
Jason, son of my brother: would you accept the crown?

JASON [*kneeling*]:
With all humility, if you and the gods decree—

PELIAS:
We do, beloved nephew, we do. It is only right.
Ah, what a blessing it is, to finally rid myself of this
burden that has lain so heavy on me for so many years.

[*He removes his crown and seems to offer it to* JASON.]

Only one thing:

[*He takes it back.*]

The devotion of my people
is so very great, they may refuse this passing of the crown—
take up arms against you—the gods forbid. Therefore
to prove your worthiness to all, do me this one service I ask—
or I should say I offer: a valiant undertaking.

JASON:
An . . . undertaking?

[*Music. During the following a second pair of servants enter. One carries a little box with two small figurines in it, Phrixus and Helle, as well as some white, powdery dust. The other carries a slender vertical pole, crowned by the golden ram. They gently illustrate the various events of* PELIAS's *story as it unfolds.*]

PELIAS:

You know the old tale of our kinsman little Phrixus and his sister
    Helle?
How they were hated and abused by their cruel stepmother,
so long ago?

JASON:
Yes.

PELIAS:
She so befuddled their father that he believed
his own little children cursed, the crops destroyed, turned to dust
by them, when it was her doing all along. She bribed the oracles
to command him to kill Phrixus and Helle.

JASON:
Unimaginable.

PELIAS:
Indeed, but just as he was dragging them
to the sacrificial site and drawing his knife,
a shadow passed overhead.

JASON:
The ram.

PELIAS:
Yes, the marvelous golden ram with wings.
Sent by the heavens in their mercy. It alit,
each of its delicate hooves raising a little cloud of dust.
Those children understood and climbed aboard
while everyone stood stony with wonder.
And it carried them up through the sky like a second sun.

JASON:
I know it well.

PELIAS:
For seven days and nights they rode eastward, far beyond
where any Greek has traveled to this day. Phrixus held the horns,
and poor Helle held him, until, giddy at the height, exhausted,
she lost her hold and fell into the sea.

As for Phrixus, he landed
in Colchis, and there the savage King Aeëtes
slew him, a crime to make the Sun avert his face,
then slew the ram itself and keeps its Fleece on display,
a reminder to all of his arrogance and power.

[One of the servants detaches the golden ram from its pole and fastens it to a cord that draws it up high above the action, where it will linger for the rest of the act. The second pair of servants exits.]

JASON:
I know the tale.

PELIAS:
It's no mere story to me, Nephew.
Every night when I close my eyes, I see our kinsman
slaughtered by that man, Aeëtes. But I am old,
and my only remaining son is far too young
for sea voyaging. I turn to you, my nephew.
Go there! Bring back the Golden Fleece.

[Music ends. Pause.]

JASON:
How could I refuse?

PELIAS [*suddenly steely*]:
Indeed, how could you? Since your king commands you. [*Friendly again and rapid*] Gather a crew from far and wide, all the heroes and strong men you like. Think of it, Jason—to sail so far beyond where anyone has ever sailed, the open water, the unknown sea. And when you return, covered in glory, this kingdom shall be yours.

JASON:
I thank you for this privilege and shall endeavor to do my best.

PELIAS:
Farewell, beloved nephew. May all the gods bless you and guide you.

JASON:
Farewell.

[JASON *leaves.* PELIAS *instantly drops his affected weakness.*]

PELIAS [*gleeful, vicious*]:
He's dead. If the sea doesn't get him or the monsters of the sea, then King Aeëtes will stick a knife in him the moment he lands.

CEPHEUS:
But what about the Fleece? How will you get it if Jason dies?

PELIAS:
Who gives a fuck about the Fleece? Are you serious? Some stinking piece of wool that's been rotting in the rain for twenty years? Thanks for the idea, by the way. Bring me those pills!

HALLWAY

[*Drums.* JASON *is striding through the hallway of Pelias's palace followed by* ATHENA. HERA *is above.*]

HERA:
Jason was no idiot. His reason told him—

ATHENA:
Pelias is out to kill you. He expects this expedition to end in ruin.

JASON:
But what can I do? Stir up the people, begin a rebellion?
If I'd wanted to do that I could have tried it long ago.

ATHENA:
Will you attempt the expedition?

JASON:
What other choice remains?

[PELIAS'S·SON *enters bouncing a ball. He is an arrogant little boy. He cannot see or hear* ATHENA.]

PELIAS'S SON:
Who are you?

JASON:
I am Jason, son of Aeson. And you?

PELIAS'S SON:
King Pelias is my father. That makes you my cousin.

ATHENA [*urgently, to* JASON]:
Make use of this.

PELIAS'S SON:
What did he want with you?

ATHENA:
Think how this could help protect you and the crew.

JASON:
Well, he's sending me off on a great voyage.

PELIAS'S SON:
He is?

ATHENA:
Careful now—use your cunning.

JASON:
One that may bring honor to us all.

ATHENA:
Good!

PELIAS'S SON [*wildly excited*]:
To who? Who is going? Who? Who gets to go?

JASON:
All sorts of heroes. As soon as word gets out, it will be the greatest company ever assembled: demigods and warriors from across the land. Who would miss the chance to sail out into the unknown world, across the open sea, to find new lands, treasure, and glory, to make a name for himself forever?

PELIAS'S SON:
I want to come!

ATHENA:
Yes!

PELIAS'S SON:
Let me ask my father.

ATHENA:
No!

JASON:
Oh no, don't do that. He'd never let you go. He'd lock you up if you were even to mention your desire.

PELIAS'S SON:
Oh.

JASON:
Don't mention it. Be reconciled. You're just a little, little boy. Be content to watch us from your walls tomorrow as we set sail. At dawn. From the eastern dock.

ATHENA:
Now turn your back.

JASON:
Farewell.

[JASON *begins to leave.*]

ATHENA:
Don't look back.

PELIAS'S SON:
Farewell.

ATHENA:
Don't look back, don't look back, don't look back.

[JASON *and* PELIAS'S SON *are both gone.* ATHENA *is triumphant, excited;* HERA, *more irritated.*]

HERA:
Daughter of Zeus! Did you notice how that old raccoon failed to mention the dangers of the trip? The monsters and the clashing rocks and all the rest of it?

ATHENA:
Indeed.

HERA:
Not even a passing reference to the dragon who guards the Golden Fleece, the dragon who never sleeps.

ATHENA:
We'll take it as it comes. I'm off to King Argos.

[ATHENA *rises in the air.*]

I'll command him to build a ship for our Jason such as no one's ever seen—a ship worthy of the open sea! And you, spread the news of the adventure throughout Achaea and Macedon, so that worthy men may join him. I'm off!

HERA:

All was done as the goddesses proclaimed. Athena herself helped build the ship, and from far and wide, down to the shore they came: heroes and demigods. The crowds cheered and rejoiced to hear each one declare his name and desire to sail with the *Argo*.

ROLL CALL

[*The audience hears the approach of drums, of men shouting excitedly. The company fills the stage, chanting and clapping. Many play various percussive instruments. They chant a nonsense phrase, such as "Sha-boo-ya! Ya! Ya! Sha-boo-ya, roll call!" until the first Argonaut steps forward to introduce himself. The drumming and rhythmic clapping continues throughout. At the end of each phrase of a given Argonaut's boast—except for* TIPHYS's *third phrase—the entire company shouts, "Yeah!" or "Roll call!" as indicated in italics below. The whole thing should be riotous, aggressive, and fast.*]

ALL:
Sha-boo-ya! Ya! Ya! Sha-boo-ya, roll call!
Sha-boo-ya! Ya! Ya! Sha-boo-ya, roll call!

IDMON:
My name is Idmon.
            Yeah!
I see the future,
            Yeah!
but don't forget that
            Yeah!

I could also hurt you.
            Roll call!

I may be blind,
            Yeah!
but I speak prophecy.
            Yeah!
And furthermore
            Yeah!
I can row the open sea.
            Roll call!

ALL:
Sha-boo-ya! Ya! Ya! Sha-boo-ya, roll call!
Sha-boo-ya! Ya! Ya! Sha-boo-ya, roll call!

MELEAGER:
Don't mispronounce it,
            Yeah!
my name's Meleager.
            Yeah!
When I see that Fleece,
            Yeah!
I'll go and seize her.
            Roll call!

When it comes to battle,
            Yeah!
no one's more eager.
            Yeah!
When you're in trouble,
            Yeah!

just shout, "Meleager!"
                    Roll call!

ALL:
Sha-boo-ya! Ya! Ya! Sha-boo-ya, roll call!
Sha-boo-ya! Ya! Ya! Sha-boo-ya, roll call!

CASTOR:
We are Castor
                    Yeah!

POLLUX:
and Pollux too.
                    Yeah!

CASTOR AND POLLUX:
Our mom had a swan
                    Yeah!
and had us two.
                    Roll call!

CASTOR:
Our father's Zeus.
                    Yeah!

POLLUX:
We can fly in the sky.
                    Yeah!

CASTOR:
We want adventure,
                    Yeah!

CASTOR AND POLLUX:
but we don't know why.
                    Roll call!

ALL:
Sha-boo-ya! Ya! Ya! Sha-boo-ya, roll call!
Sha-boo-ya! Ya! Ya! Sha-boo-ya, roll call!

TIPHYS:
You'll need a pilot,
                    Yeah!
and that is I.
                    Yeah!
My name is Tiphys—

the stars are my guide.
                    Roll call!

Through wind and waves
                    Yeah!
I'll bring her through.
                    Yeah!
My name's Tiphys,
                    Yeah!
now how 'bout you?
                    Roll call!

ALL:
Sha-boo-ya! Ya! Ya! Sha-boo-ya, roll call!
Sha-boo-ya! Ya! Ya! Sha-boo-ya, roll call!

HERCULES:
My name is Hercules.

       Yeah!

I've done a dozen deeds,

       Yeah!

so no one better not . . . because . . .

       Yeah!

              um . . .

[*It falls apart.* HERCULES *has no rhythm.*]

I'm Hercules!

       Yeah!

I'm Hercules!

       Yeah!

Hercules! Hercules! Hercules!

[*The percussive rhythm picks itself up and carries on softly under the following as* HERCULES *struts around, striking his chest, showing his muscles, bellowing his own name, and so on. The company is unaware of the goddesses.*]

HERA [*furiously*]:
What's that idiot doing here?

ATHENA:
Let it go, he's a brilliant warrior.

HERCULES:
Hercules!

HERA:

Brilliant? Him? He doesn't have a thought in his head! He's a baked potato!

HERCULES:

I'm Hercules!

ATHENA:

Let it go.

HERA [*pouting, furiously*]:

I will not! He never does me honor!

ATHENA:

You sent snakes to strangle him in his crib!

HERA:

I hate him!

ATHENA:

And he strangled the snakes instead—at age two!—

HERCULES:

Hercules!

ATHENA:

—he's earned his place on board. Be reasonable!

HERA:

Every time I see him he reminds me of my husband's . . . wayward ways . . . with that whore!

ATHENA:
Your husband has peopled the earth with his sons—

HERCULES:
Hercules!

ATHENA:
—what's one more? Use your head.

HERA:
He drives me crazy!

[*The company comes roaring back in.*]

ALL:
        Roll call!
Sha-boo-ya! Ya! Ya! Sha-boo-ya, roll call!
Sha-boo-ya! Ya! Ya! Sha-boo-ya, roll call!

[HYLAS, *companion to* HERCULES, *steps forward. He declares himself shyly.*]

HYLAS:
My name is Hylas.
        Yeah!
I bear his arms.
        Yeah!
He killed my father:
        Yeah!
but that's long ago.
        Roll call!

We are companions
                Yeah!
under the sky,
                Yeah!
and we'll be together
                Yeah!
till the day we die.
                Roll call!

ALL:
Sha-boo-ya! Ya! Ya! Sha-boo-ya, roll call!
Sha-boo-ya! Ya! Ya! Sha-boo-ya, roll call!

ATALANTA:
My name's Atalanta.

HERCULES [*alone, belligerently*]:
Yeah?

ATALANTA:
Think I'm out of place?

HERCULES:
Yeah!

ATALANTA:
Then just one question,

HERCULES:
Yeah?

ATALANTA:
would you like to race?

ALL:
Roll call!
Sha-boo-ya! Ya! Ya! Sha-boo-ya, roll call!
Sha-boo-ya! Ya! Ya! Sha-boo-ya, roll call!

UNCLE [*pointing to* MELEAGER]:
I play his uncle
      Yeah!
and others too.
      Yeah!
For all those Argonauts—
      Yeah!

ALL [*to audience*]:
We are too few!
      Roll call!
Sha-boo-ya! Ya! Ya! Sha-boo-ya, roll call!
Sha-boo-ya! Ya! Ya! Sha-boo-ya, roll call!

JASON:
My name is Jason.
      Yeah!
I thank you all.
      Yeah!
Now let's continue
      Yeah!
with the long roll call.
      Roll call!

ALL:
Sha-boo-ya! Ya! Ya! Sha-boo-ya, roll call!
Sha-boo-ya! Ya! Ya! Sha-boo-ya, roll call!

[*The company assembles into a military formation and marches and chants the following either severally or together, very rapidly, with four strong beats per line.*]

There's Augeias and Kepheus and Amphion too,
and Talos and Klytos and Erytos who
brought Eurytion, Koronos, Kekyra—all,
and handsome Hesperre and Telamon tall,
the arrogant Idas and Iphitos from
the windy Lake Xanis: so one by one
they came to the shore, all of them, all
and cried out their names in the endless roll call.

[*They break apart with much shouting and cheering.* HERA *exits.*]

LIBATION/PROPHECY

JASON:
Friends, all the gear that's needed for fitting out a vessel
is ranged here in good order. Tomorrow we will launch.
But first, without prejudice,
let us choose the best man among us as a leader.

[*Everyone looks at* HERCULES, *who holds up his right hand. Despite the formality of his response,* HERCULES *is not bright. His speech is slow, clumsy.*]

HERCULES:
Let no man offer this honor to me: I will not consent—

[MELEAGER *begins to rise.* HERCULES *continues pointedly.*]

And further, I shall stop any other man from rising.
Let the person who mustered this host have its leadership as well.

ARGONAUTS [*enthusiastically, variously*]:
Hear hear! Jason! Our leader!

JASON:
If then you entrust me with the protection of your honor,
nothing remains to hold us from our journey.
Let us give libation to the sea.

[*Music, an ominous drone.* HYLAS *comes forward with a goblet of
wine and hands it to* JASON.]

O God, who with a nod can stir the ocean to foam,
hear our prayer and grant us your indulgence.
We are the first of mankind to venture forth on unlawful
paths across your waters, and therefore, one might suppose,
deserve the worst of your storms. Yet hear me:
It is not my own idea to presume in this way.
It is Pelias who has commanded us. His prayers are false;
do not be swayed by him. Let your waters receive me, bear me up,
and protect this ship and its crew of kings.

[ATHENA *embraces* IDMON *violently from behind. He begins to moan.*]

Idmon, what is it?

UNCLE:
He sees something.

JASON:
What is it, Idmon?

IDMON [*in the throes of a vision*]:
Poseidon has heard you and called together
the ocean's pantheon to protest our voyage
across the forbidden waters. But now Hera herself
comes to implore her mighty brother . . .
The gods of the sea have yielded! They grant permission
and say that we may sail upon the open sea!

[*Everyone shouts and cheers. But* IDMON *continues.*]

Yet I see a change in fortune. Hylas I see, but why does he cover his
hair with reeds and rushes? Why does he carry a pitcher?
And Pollux, how did you get those wounds? And Meleager, what
is your mother doing by the fire?

[*with growing terror*]

                                        Now I see bulls,
but flame comes from their snouts. They plow furrows in earth.
And helmets appear? And spears? There is the Fleece—
but who is this girl and why is she covered in blood?
Jason, save your children—!

JASON:
I have no—

IDMON:
—Carry them away—hurry!—
I see how the voyage will go: heavy toils

and heavier griefs we must bear
yet the *Argo* shall overcome and come home again!

[*Music ends as* ATHENA *releases* IDMON. *He collapses. A moment of stunned silence. Then—*]

HERCULES:
Yes! Success! Success and glory! Ar-go-nauts! Ar-go-nauts!

ARGONAUTS:
Ar-go-nauts! Ar-go-nauts!

[*The chant accelerates until it breaks apart into much chest thumping, shouting, and so on.*]

JASON:
You've heard Idmon
and know that there is hope for a happy ending.
I'll no longer dwell on the tyrant Pelias's motives;
he has done us the honor of setting us on this course,
we must embrace it as a gift—as all difficulties are—
and think of the tales we'll have to tell our grandsons!
Meanwhile, our hardships have not yet begun: Look!
We have couches of soft seaweed and the air is sweet;
the water is calm. Let us enjoy our last evening on these shores.

[*All the* ARGONAUTS *leave except* IDMON. ATHENA *is beside him.*]

ATHENA [*gently*]:
Idmon, why do you sit apart?

[*He says nothing. He is weeping.*]

What did you see?

IDMON:
You know what I saw.

ATHENA:
Say it aloud.

IDMON:
I saw my own body, lonely in the dark. Dead and far from home.

ATHENA:
You needn't get on the ship. You can stay—

IDMON:
I'm getting on that ship.

ATHENA:
But there's no reason—

IDMON [*defiantly, straightening himself*]:
Reason has no part in this. I'm getting on that ship.

[IDMON *exits.*]

LAUNCH

ATHENA:
The stars were gliding westward into the ocean's source,
and the jingle of horses' bridles were sounding in caves in the east,
where Phoebus stables his steeds. At the Hours' prompting, the Sun

put on his splendid tiara of shining rays and rose in the sky
to bedazzle the waves on the shore where the Argonauts slept.
From the town and down the mountains, everyone came, people
and creatures of all kinds, to see, at last, the launch.

[*Music, hopeful, exuberant, driving. All hands on deck. The* ARGO-
NAUTS *enter variously with rigging for the ship. One climbs up the
mast and pulls down a ring for the rigging. Some toss oarlocks to
one another and place them in the tholepins on the edge of the deck.
All busy themselves with ropes and oars. At a certain moment,
the ring around the mast is raised with all the ropes attached.
Many exit. A centaur wanders through, marveling. Birds wheel
by. Several* ARGONAUTS *reenter with their oars and climb the ladder onto the bridge above the deck. The ladder is pulled up or taken
away. Just then, at the last moment,* PELIAS'S SON *enters with his
ball and cries out.*]

PELIAS'S SON:
Wait! Wait for me!

[PELIAS'S SON *drops his ball and runs to the men who pull him up
onto the bridge. Music ends.*]

VISITATION

[*Several* ARGONAUTS, *including* JASON, *are rowing swiftly on the
bridge.* PELIAS *enters opposite and below with* CEPHEUS *and* ASTERION.]

PELIAS:
What are you saying?

38

CEPHEUS:
Most gracious—

PELIAS:
Get him back! Get my son back!

CEPHEUS:
It's impossible. The ship has launched—

ASTERION:
It is on the sea.

PELIAS:
Go to the house of Jason's parents. Make a visit to my brother and that lovely wife of his—and their new son. Go!

[CEPHEUS *and* ASTERION *exit.* PELIAS *holds his son's ball. Jason's mother,* ALCIMEDE, *enters opposite. Her infant son, a little puppet child, floats in from above. She catches him and lays him on the ground. His little arms and legs move slightly throughout the scene. She opens the trapdoor and begins her incantations. Vapors rise through the trapdoor. All this while* PELIAS *continues.*]

Oh my boy, are you grieving for me now as I grieve for you?
Jason tricked you, I know, to revenge himself on me.
Oh, Jason, you think that you are safe?
You may have my son in your sights, but I have your father in mine!

[*Jason's father,* AESON, *enters. The* ARGONAUTS, *still above, row much more slowly throughout the rest of the scene.*]

AESON:
My lovely, what are you doing?

ALCIMEDE:
Oh Aeson, I think I've done everything right:
I've poured the ox blood and added all the herbs,
and I've said the spell backward and forward now—
to imitate the way Charon goes—back and forth across the river—

AESON:
But why—

ALCIMEDE:
I am summoning your father from the underworld,
to tell us of our boy's fate.

AESON:
Come away from there, my Alcimede, we need no spirits
to know that Jason will return to embrace us once again.

ALCIMEDE:
How could he go and leave me here, to gaze out at the empty sea
day after day—

AESON:
                              He had no choice: my brother has
done this in his hatred and his fear. Come away from there—
I know you want to believe in such things, but—

[*Suddenly the* GHOST *rises through the trapdoor.*]

GHOST:
Do not be afraid! Jason is well. He flies over the blue water
drawing ever closer to Colchis. He will arrive,
the terror of nations, and return with glorious spoils

and a Colchian bride as well. But if I could, I would come
back even to the sorrow of life to prevent what will happen then . . .

[*The* GHOST *seems to sink away then suddenly rises again.*]

                         Meanwhile, your brother has
murder in his heart. Flee for your lives! Or free
yourselves from your enfeebled limbs by your own hand.
Hurry! Escape! Or die disgraced at your brother's hand.
The throngs of the dead call out to you.

[*The* GHOST *disappears.*]

AESON:
Be steady. Whatever happens I am by your side.
I will not deign to prolong my life or look upon
Jason's face unless it be with you.

ALCIMEDE:
We shall not die at the hand of your brother
who has so hurt our son. Nor shall we run from him.

AESON:
We are in agreement then?

[*She nods and goes off.* AESON *prays.*]

                         My beloved father,
summoned as you have been to witness my death,
welcome us now to your dim and quiet world. And I pray you
attend on Pelias now, my long-ago brother.
Visit him with fear. Let him walk the shore and worry
and all his schemes for protection be endless and all in vain.

Let his end be shameful, secret, and wretched.
This is my dying prayer: that he be made to pay
for having sent my firstborn son and his brave companions to sea.

[ALCIMEDE *returns with two cups of poison.*]

ALCIMEDE:
Are you ready, sir?

AESON:
Are you?

ALCIMEDE:
I am. Only the baby ...

AESON:
We've always known. The plans are ready, and Aulos and Ancaeus
know just what to do. But, my lovely, we must hurry.

ALCIMEDE:
All right then.

AESON:
All right.

[*They raise their cups to each other.*]

ALCIMEDE:
Forever.

AESON:
Forever.

[*They drink, just as shouting and pounding begin offstage.*]

CEPHEUS AND ASTERION [*variously*]:
Let us in! King Pelias's men!

[CEPHEUS *and* ASTERION *enter as* AESON *and* ALCIMEDE *collapse.*
CEPHEUS *and* ASTERION *look at the empty cups then see the baby.
One goes over to tickle it. The other comes and catches all its strings
in one hand and severs them with a knife. They leave. Music.*]

ATHENA:
Far below, removed from the world of light, is the deep
realm of Hades. It is said there are two doors through which
our shades may enter, one of which stands open
all the time, and men may enter, entire nations,
and even the greatest kings.

[PELIAS *exits through one open door. Throughout the following,* AL-
CIMEDE *and* AESON *slowly rise.* ALCIMEDE *gathers the baby in her
arms, and they approach the second door, which gently, slowly
opens as they near. A great light shines through it.*]

                    The other, no one attempts
or tries to unbar, but now and again it opens
spontaneously, flies wide to receive a rare person:
someone who never lied, or spoke ill of anyone,
who loved the children of others as he loved his own.
Into this realm of sunlight Aeson leads his wife and son.
They pause for a moment to peer through the other door,
where monstrous creatures lurk at the threshold.
Awesome, those dreadful specters, and awesome but utterly different
these precincts of blessing, ease, and joy.

[AESON *carries* ALCIMEDE, *like a bride, across the threshold of the second door. Music shifts.*]

BOREAS

[*The* ARGONAUTS *immediately increase their rowing speed, but during the following lines of* ATHENA, *they descend from the bridge and set about business onboard. A sail drops in along the mast and is spread out. Other* ARGONAUTS *enter and busy themselves about the ship, checking rigging and so on.*]

ATHENA:
Meanwhile, unaware of these crimes, Jason slices his way
through the waves. All the heroes pull together, their arms
gleaming in the sun, keeping time as they push through the
white sea foam. When at last they clear the headland, Tiphys
gives the order to raise the sail, and immediately it catches
the freshening breeze. But now Boreas, god of the winds,
stirs in his cave.

[BOREAS *appears in a window above. He has a little model of the* Argo *in his hands, which he will soon begin to abuse. Music fades or ends.*]

BOREAS:
Daughter of Zeus!

HERCULES [*feeling the ship lurch*]:
What's that?

44

JASON:
Not used to sailing? That's the breath of the ocean.

HERCULES:
Make it stop!

[*The Argo* pitches back and forth. All the ARGONAUTS *are tossed from one side of the ship to the other, rolling in and out of the doors which open and slam shut throughout the following.*]

BOREAS:
Daughter of Zeus!

HERCULES:
It's getting worse!

ATHENA:
Boreas! Take your winds back to their cave! Go home!

BOREAS:
I see it myself! A wooden thing, with cloth to entrap me.

ATHENA:
Calm down!

HERCULES:
I don't feel good.

ATHENA:
I built the mast myself!

HERCULES:
Where is the sun going? What's all those clouds?

BOREAS:
I may not stir the sea from the bottom, but still
I have the power to destroy their presumptuous vessel!

ATHENA:
We have permission!

BOREAS:
Permission of Poseidon, not of me.

HERCULES [*shouting to the sky*]:
Stop it—I warn you! I'll shoot my arrows at you!

ATHENA:
Listen to me, Boreas!

HERCULES:
I'm going to throw my spear!

ATHENA:
Your time is over! After this, vessels will pass this way and that
from Pharos and Tyre and everyone take for granted this strange thing.

HYLAS:
We're taking water!

UNCLE:
The yardarm is catching crabs!

BOREAS:
Let me destroy them, or I swear, I will make widows and orphans
for a thousand years! And then a thousand more!

ATHENA:
You won't destroy this ship!

BOREAS:
And they will curse me from now on!

ATHENA:
Enough! I say enough! Send your winds back.
It is time you submit to the craft of men—to sails.

[BOREAS *departs with a cry. The sea calms. The* ARGONAUTS *are all clinging to the rigging and the mast.*]

TIPHYS:
Courage my friends! You see the clear sky overhead—
and Cynthia's moon with her delicate horns has appeared—
pure white, no tinge of red at all!

IDMON:
We have survived our first storm!

HERCULES:
There'll be more?

JASON:
Tiphys, you've brought us through.

TIPHYS [*looking toward* ATHENA]:
It was not I alone: Athena taught me my craft,
and it is with her help we have survived.

ANDROMEDA

[*Music. The* ARGONAUTS *take up their rowing positions, either on the bridge or on the deck. During the following, there is some little action that illustrates the adventures.*]

ATHENA:
                        So on they voyaged,
running before the wind. Through the night
the stars were their guide. By day
they raised the sail and peered at the vanishing coast.
Two more days they traveled bearing north and east.

                        Soon they came upon
Samothrace, Electra's island, home of the cult of the Thracian
rites. The priest came down and greeted them, showed them
the temple, and explained the mysteries, but no one may
ever speak of these without calling down a curse, and so,
out of respect, and reverence, we must omit these from our tale.

                              The sun rose up and sank in the sky,
and then, for the first time since the world began,
a ship from foreign parts pulled up to foreign shores.

JASON:
Men, we've toiled hard today and earned a rest.
Let's use the sails as tents and make our camp.

[*The* ARGONAUTS *disperse except for* HERCULES *and* HYLAS, *who are up on the bridge. A large green cloth for the sea covers the stage.*]

ATHENA:
But Hercules was not tired and went to walk along the shore
with his constant friend, his Hylas.

[ANDROMEDA, *tied to the mast, which is now a tree on the cliffside,
moans.*]

HERCULES:
What's that?

HYLAS:
What?

[ANDROMEDA *moans a little louder.*]

HERCULES:
That noise?

HYLAS:
It's just the sea. But it's getting awfully dark.
Perhaps we should—

ANDROMEDA [*in a very small voice*]:
Help me!

HERCULES:
That. Do you hear it?

HYLAS:
I'm not . . . sure . . . It's pitch-black!

ANDROMEDA:
Save me! Someone, help!

HERCULES:
There it is—there. Look down on the cliff.

[ANDROMEDA *moans.*]

HYLAS:
I think it's a girl—she's all tied up.

HERCULES:
Hey, miss! Miss! What are you doing there?
What have you done that someone should bind you up like that?

ANDROMEDA:
Oh sir! I'm guiltless—I swear! Quick! Help me!

HERCULES:
But what have you done?

ANDROMEDA:
I tell you—nothing! Listen! Years ago a plague
descended on our city, and then
enormous waves arose from the sea, and with them
a terrible sea monster. The priests of Ammon said
that every year a maiden must be sacrificed to it, and
this year I, Andromeda, am the one.

HERCULES:
A sea monster?

ANDROMEDA:
Sir, my father has declared a great prize for anyone
that saves me and rids us of the monster:
a pair of dazzling snow-white horses!

HERCULES:
Horses? I'm with a boat right now.

ANDROMEDA:
Oh sir, they are a marvel! Surely you are the one
intended for this task! Please!

HERCULES:
Well . . .

[*The waves begin to roil. Part of the green sea cloth rises. Someone
attaches a pair of eyes to it, and in this way, the monster materializes.*]

ANDROMEDA:
Oh, here it is! It's coming!

HYLAS:
Hercules, look below!

ANDROMEDA:
                    EEEEEEEEEE!

HERCULES:
Stop that shrieking! Now he sees you!

ANDROMEDA:
EEEEEEEEEE!

HERCULES:
                    Hylas! That stone! Be quick!
O Father Zeus, aid me in this venture. Let my aim
be true; bless my weapons and—[*to* HYLAS] Would you hurry up!

HYLAS [*struggling mightily with the stone*]:
It's too heavy!

ANDROMEDA:
EEEEEEEEEEEE!

HERCULES:
Move over!

[HERCULES *lifts the stone as though it weighed nothing.*]

HYLAS:
                              Watch out! It's coming!

HERCULES:
Go back to where you came from, you worm!
You treacherous beast!

[*He brains the monster with the stone. The eyeballs fly into the air. The monster evaporates, and the green cloth disappears down the trapdoor.*]

Ha ha! That'll teach you! Think you can get the best of Hercules!

ANDROMEDA:
Untie me!

HERCULES [*to* HYLAS]:
Did you see that? Did you see that?

HYLAS:
I saw! I witnessed what you did! Who will
ever forget it!

ANDROMEDA:
Sirs! Untie me please!

HERCULES:
Go on down, Hylas! Untie her now. That monster's done for good!
He'll not come back to trouble us or anyone! Hercules!

ANDROMEDA:
Thank you, sirs! Oh thank you! Follow me home!

HERCULES:
No. I'm with the *Argo* now, we're bound for other shores
and can provide for no horses onboard.

ANDROMEDA:
You must come back some day and claim your prize!
Until then may the gods bless you and keep you forever!
Farewell!

[*She runs off.* JASON *and several* ARGONAUTS *enter, passing her.*]

JASON:
Hercules, who was that girl? What are you doing here
all covered with sea foam and brine? We missed you at camp,
and just then the sea came up, and the sky grew black—

HERCULES:
We'll tell you all about it! Hylas saw it! We'll tell you
all about it.

53

ATHENA:
And you can bet he did.

WOMEN OF LEMNOS

[*Music. The* ARGONAUTS *take up their rowing positions.* ATHENA *stands in front of the mast.*]

ATHENA:
At last they cleared the straits
and the dome of sea and sky opened up.
They saw a whole new world. On a rocky shore
an old soldier who lay dead was so astonished
to see a Grecian ship that he sat up to watch
it pass. Two more days they voyaged, and then . . .

[*Music ends. The* ARGONAUTS *peer forward toward the shore; the* FIRST, SECOND, *and* THIRD WOMAN OF LEMNOS *peer back at them. Neither group can see the other clearly or hear each other.*]

CASTOR:
What's that?

FIRST WOMAN OF LEMNOS:
What's that?

JASON:
An island?

SECOND WOMAN OF LEMNOS:
Do you think it is the Thracians?

FIRST WOMAN OF LEMNOS:
The gods forbid.

JASON:
Are those warriors lining the coast?

THIRD WOMAN OF LEMNOS:
Should we hide?

TIPHYS:
No, no—

FIRST WOMAN OF LEMNOS:
No, no—the sail is not Thracian.

TIPHYS:
They're beardless and carry no arms.

JASON:
Amazons?

SECOND WOMAN OF LEMNOS:
Strangers?

HERCULES:
No ... they aren't Amazons, I can tell you that.

FIRST WOMAN OF LEMNOS:
Quickly, gather everyone together.

[*The* FIRST, SECOND, *and* THIRD WOMAN OF LEMNOS *exit.*]

UNCLE:
What should we do?

JASON:
As your leader I should
be the first to volunteer. I will go ashore,
carrying the olive branch, and discover what kind of
folk live here—gentle or savage. There is a chance
we might gain provisions, or at least a night's rest onshore.
Who among you will join me?

IDMON:
I will.

POLLUX [*approaching with an olive branch*]:
And I.

CASTOR [*not to be outdone*]:
And I as well!

JASON:
Let's not overwhelm them with too strong a force: Castor,
be content to let your brother go.

[*The* FIRST, THIRD, *and* FOURTH WOMAN OF LEMNOS *enter.*]

FIRST WOMAN OF LEMNOS:
Ladies, what shall we do? Even now I see
three of their company coming to shore.

FOURTH WOMAN OF LEMNOS:
Send them away at once!

THIRD WOMAN OF LEMNOS:
We can have no visitors—

FOURTH WOMAN OF LEMNOS:
No prying eyes!

FIRST WOMAN OF LEMNOS:
But wait. Since . . . since what happened . . . happened—
You know it's true! All our virgins are growing white haired.
The streets are silent—no cries of children. We can't
continue as we have—

FOURTH WOMAN OF LEMNOS:
                         It's too risky!

THIRD WOMAN OF LEMNOS:
What would we tell them when they ask after the men?

ATHENA:
Indeed. What had happened to the men?

[*Music. During the following song,* JASON, IDMON, *and* POLLUX *take the parts of the men of Lemnos. Little actions illustrate the events of the song. The women use their headscarves first as sewing or scrubbing cloths, then as binding on the wrists of the girls of Thrace, as strangling cords, as blood and tears, and so on.*]

ATHENA [*speaking*]:
The women of Lemnos were once like others,
happy enough in their lives with their men.

The women of Lemnos
      were once like others,
happy enough in their lives with their men.

Then over the water
      the men went sailing
and raided and captured the girls of Thrace.

As they sailed homeward,
      the men all rejoiced,
"How happy our wives will be with their men—

freed from their chores
      by those spoils of war
the hapless and captured girls of Thrace."

ATHENA [*speaking*]:
But Rumor came down, banished from heaven,
to bother the earth with her whispering lies.

SINGERS:
But Rumor came down,
      banished from heaven,
to bother the earth with her whispering lies.

She whispered to one,
      and then to another,
that those girls had stolen the hearts of the men.

She said, "They cast off
      their love with the hawsers
when they set out to sail away from their wives.

Those scented young girls
have captured their captors' hearts from their wives."

ATHENA [*speaking*]:
The wives believed Rumor.

SINGERS:
Oh love you have left me
      while I was here waiting.
You traded my heart for a handful of straw.

How can we sing this—
      please close your eyes—
The horror of what happened next with those wives.

Madness had seized them,
      they loomed in the doorways:
The men found death at the hands of their wives.

Then the male children
      and grandfathers too
the uncles and brothers all lost their lives.

Then Rumor departed
      and left them all groaning
to see what they'd done to their own sorry lives.

Oh love you have left me
      while I was here waiting.
I traded our love for a handful of straw.

[*Song ends. Long pause.*]

THIRD WOMAN OF LEMNOS:
We can't tell them that.

FIRST WOMAN OF LEMNOS:
No. But sisters, nonetheless we need these men,
if only temporarily—

[JASON, IDMON, *and* POLLUX *approach. The women can barely disguise their excitement.*]

Gentlemen!
We see you carry the olive branch and welcome you:
please enter our city in friendship.

JASON:
We are honored, madame.

FIRST WOMAN OF LEMNOS:
We are the women of Lemnos. May we inquire
as to who you are and where you come from?

JASON:
Jason of Iolcos, the leader of our crew. That is
the *Argo* you see in your harbor. Madame, we
have had rough sailing and we wish to know
whether we might beg shelter for a night.

FIRST WOMAN OF LEMNOS:
Only one? Sailors, this is no season for being on the sea.
The storms are frequent now. Why not stay with us a while?

THIRD WOMAN OF LEMNOS:
Bring the whole crew.

FIRST WOMAN OF LEMNOS:
Enjoy our hospitality. Only one thing—we hope you
will not mind—there are no men here at all, not
one to welcome you and entertain you as they should.
They abandoned us long ago for the sake of some captive girls
they took from Thrace, and they stole our children too.
It's only us. Alone.

[*The* FIRST, THIRD, *and* FOURTH WOMAN OF LEMNOS *lead the eager*
JASON, IDMON, *and* POLLUX *off. We hear the sounds of merry-*
making. Throughout the following, other ARGONAUTS *sneak off the*
ship to join them, first singly, then in pairs, urgent.]

ATHENA:
⠀⠀⠀⠀⠀⠀⠀⠀⠀⠀⠀⠀⠀⠀They lingered. Each of them,
one by one, came from the ship to shore.
Days and nights passed, then weeks and even months.
Those ladies of Lemnos had not forgotten their charms.
Only one stayed behind, with his companion,
refusing to leave the ship.

HERCULES [*entering with* HYLAS]:
Is this what we signed up for? There weren't enough weddings
in our native lands so we had to go and seek some more?
Not enough drink and fine dining?

[*To* HYLAS] Go. Fetch the crew here
for an hour—if you can pry them from their beds.

ATHENA:
So one by one they came from the shore to the ship.

[*The men come forward, straightening their clothes, abashed, limping, exhausted from their time with the women.*]

HERCULES:
                                    Jason, tell us now:
Have you forgotten why you gathered this crew?
Was it to snuggle up with a passel of foreign women?
Myself, I heard it was to find the Golden Fleece
and capture it and bring it home. But if you
have changed your mind and decided to stay
here instead and populate this island and
get yourself talked about, then let me know
and we'll be on our way.

[*The women come forward for a tearful, clinging farewell. One of them is knitting baby clothes.* HERCULES *will have none of it.*]

ATHENA:
                                    Thus he spoke,
and the crew knew that he was right. The next
morning they bade farewell.

HERCULES

HERCULES:
Come on, men! Enough of this! I challenge you all to a contest:
who can row the fastest?

ARGONAUTS [*resigned, taking up their positions at the oars*]:
All right . . . all right . . .

HERCULES:
I wonder who the winner will be? Hah!
Ready? One . . . two . . . threefourfive GO!

[HERA *wanders in as the* ARGONAUTS *frantically row.*]

What, can't keep up! Better hurry there! Grip your oars, mates,
like I gripped those snakes old Hera sent to kill me in my crib!
Is it my fault—faster there! Faster!—Is it my fault she can't keep
her husband at home? Hah! I was only—

ARGONAUTS [*having heard this before*]:
Two years old.

HERCULES:
That's right! Only two years old and I strangled those
snakes! I'm the fastest! I'm the fastest! I'm the—

[HERA *snaps his oar in half.*]

GOD DAMN IT! GOD FUCKING DAMN IT!
I WAS FUCKING WINNING! FUCKING—

JASON [*as* HERCULES *continues to rage*]:
No man can deny it, Hercules. The contest is yours.

HERCULES [*triumphant, but hardly calm*]:
HERCULES!

JASON:
Let's make landfall for the night. Look, the coast ahead is
dark with forest—surely you can find timber for a new oar
—an even better one.

HERCULES:
Are they tall? Tall enough?

JASON:
Are what tall enough?

HERCULES:
THE TREES.

JASON:
Yes, yes, they're tall.

HERCULES:
I need a tall one!

JASON:
Yes, yes.

ATHENA:
They put in for the night.

[HERCULES *and* HYLAS *linger as the* ARGONAUTS *disperse,* MELEAGER *leading* IDMON. HERA *watches and schemes.*]

HERCULES:
Hylas, I'm heading east. There looks to be
strong timber there, and there is daylight enough.
Go fetch the pitcher and fill it up
with water from one of the mountain streams,
then come back to shore, make camp, and wait for me.

ATHENA:
So off they went, each in his own direction, thinking
nothing of this parting, so much like any other.

IDMON [*pausing*]:
Is Hylas carrying a pitcher?

MELEAGER:
Yes, what of it?

IDMON:
Nothing, it's . . . nothing.

[IDMON *and* MELEAGER *leave.*]

ATHENA:
That's just the way it happens, isn't it? Unbearable loss.
It doesn't announce itself. Like as not, there are no portents:
the birds fly aimless in the air, not forming patterns,
the stars glide by in their timeless course—
nothing out of place, right up to the very edge.

[HYLAS *has arrived at the edge of a stream.* DRYOPE, *a water nymph,*
emerges.]

DRYOPE:
Who are you, handsome boy?

HYLAS:
My name is Hylas.

DRYOPE:
And where do you come from, Mr. Hylas?

HYLAS:
From . . . all over, I guess. Um . . .

DRYOPE:
This is my stream you disturb.

HYLAS:
Oh—I'm sorry. I . . . I didn't mean to.

DRYOPE:
You're so beautiful. Won't you come closer,
that I may look at you.

HYLAS:
No, I think . . .

DRYOPE:
Come closer.

HYLAS:
I'd best be returning—

DRYOPE:
Closer.

[*Suddenly she pulls him in. He cries out as he disappears.* HERCULES
reenters dragging half a tree.]

HERCULES:
This should do.

[POLYPHEMUS *runs on, out of breath, carrying a lantern and very frightened.*]

POLYPHEMUS:
Hercules—

HERCULES:
What's wrong with you?

POLYPHEMUS:
I—

[*He stops.*]

HERCULES:
Speak up! What do you have to say?

POLYPHEMUS:
Hylas went to the spring as you told him—

HERCULES:
Yes?

POLYPHEMUS:
And—I dread to be the first—

HERCULES:
Tell me!

POLYPHEMUS:
to bring you bitter tidings—

HERCULES:
Tell me!

POLYPHEMUS:
Hylas went to the spring, but he's not come back in safety.

HERCULES:
What do you mean?

POLYPHEMUS:
We heard him cry out, and then nothing. We went to the spring,
but he wasn't there. He's not anywhere—we've looked and looked.

HERCULES:
What kind of cry was it?

POLYPHEMUS:
It—

HERCULES:
WHAT KIND OF CRY?

POLYPHEMUS:
Terror. It was a cry of terror. Perhaps some wild beasts got him
or savages—

HERCULES [*calling*]:
Hylas! [*To* POLYPHEMUS] Where was this spring? [*Calling*] Hylas!

POLYPHEMUS:
A mile this way—to the west.

HERCULES [*calling*]:
Hylas! Hylas!

[*As* HERCULES *searches frantically, the other* ARGONAUTS *enter.*]

ATHENA:
All night long he searched—and found nothing.

HERCULES:
Hylas! Where are you?

ATHENA:
He ran through the woods. All day
and the next day as well, and then two more.

HERCULES:
Hylas? Do you hear me? Answer me! Answer me, Hylas!

JASON:
Hercules, we must set sail. The wind is behind us now.
All of us have searched and prayed, offered sacrifice—nothing.

HERCULES:
I'm not leaving.

JASON:
For three days now. The crew, I don't know that I—

HERCULES:
I'm not leaving without him. Hylas! Hylas! Answer me.

ATHENA:
And he disappeared deep, deep into the woods.

[*The* ARGONAUTS *are waiting, frustrated, bored.*]

MELEAGER:
Now we've waited a week with south wind blowing behind us!
We could have beached on Colchis by now were it not for that moron.
What are we doing here?

UNCLE:
                                                    Nephew, we can't abandon him!
Who else is as strong—and strong of heart?

MELEAGER:
He is a son of Zeus, but Castor and Pollux here can boast
the same. And look at me! When I was born the gods
decreed my life would last only as long as the log then
burning in the fire, but my mother, in her wisdom,
snatched that log away and locked it up. I have
a share in immortality even Hercules can't claim,
and I hereby give my solemn pledge to follow
and serve you, Jason, in any fight we may face, any manner of foe—

UNCLE:
What's this talk of loyalty when you're ready to leave
a comrade behind?

IDMON:
                                    And not just any comrade—
Where were these boasts when Hercules was here?

MELEAGER:
Who here really thinks the big hero is coming back?
The queen of heaven hates him! Can he still be alive?

70

JASON:
He may ...

MELEAGER:
Then where is he? A madness has overwhelmed his mind—
or perhaps he's finally thought twice about sharing his fame
with the likes of us.

[*Pause.*]

POLLUX:
Well, we have waited seven days ...

CASTOR:
Hylas was pleasant enough, but ...

TIPHYS:
It's true. Why isn't he here? If he could be, he would.
He must be dead—or run mad.

ATHENA:
It was decided.

[*The* ARGONAUTS *depart as* HERCULES *enters, holding Hylas's pitcher.*
HERA *relishes in his distress.*]

HERCULES:
O Hera, queen of heaven, I know this is your work.
Your husband loved my mother—so long ago and still
it drives you mad. It has no end, no end.
You sent two serpents to kill me in my crib
—would that they had managed
and made my swaddling clothes a shroud.

Oh Hylas, how can I leave you here alone,
lost on this barren hillside? What do all of my adventures,
all my glorious deeds, mean without you to witness them?

ATHENA [to HERA]:
Are you satisfied? The hero of Tiryns is going mad,
and his faithless comrades have sailed away from him
and left him on this desolate shore!

HERA:
He never did me honor.

ATHENA:
Look at him!

HERA:
He's none of my concern.

ATHENA:
He doesn't even know what's happened!

[HERA exits.]

Sleep, Hercules.

[ATHENA waves her hand over HERCULES and he instantly falls asleep.
Music. HYLAS rises from the stream, wearing a crown of vines and
flowers. HERCULES seems to wake. Throughout the following, the
ARGONAUTS depart in the distance, the ship growing smaller.]

HERCULES:
Hylas?

HYLAS:

Don't mourn for me, dear friend, don't turn your face from the sun.
All my life this stream has been awaiting me. It was my fate—
there's nothing we can do. Blame Hera, if you must,
or the nymph that stole me away from you—
but look, she has given me love, and the honor of her watery court.
I've put down my bow and quiver now, and all the joys of the hunt.
The world has turned, dear friend, it is another day.

                                          Listen to me,
our comrades have undone the mooring cables—it's true—
and sailed away. The ship is growing ever smaller on the
horizon. They've left you all alone on this island.
It was Meleager who convinced them, and for this, one day
he shall be punished when his own mother does to him
what you might right now long to do.

                                        Awake, arise,
and be brave in the face of life's adversity.
One day you shall ascend to the heavens where the stars shall bear
  you high.
Until then, let my love provide you with strength and comfort.
O friend, remember me.

[HYLAS *sinks away. The music ends.* HERCULES *seems unable to move.*]

ATHENA:

                              Hercules. Hey. Have you thought
lately of those snow-white horses promised you by that girl—
the one tied out there on the cliffs?

HERCULES:

Horses?

ATHENA:
They're waiting for you now, growing fat in their stables.
Wait, wait! I think I hear them. They're neighing . . .
"Where's Hercules? Where's our new master? We can't
wait to be with him—

[HERCULES *is amused in spite of himself.*]

What adventure he will show us. How proudly we will bear
him through the streets as all the world comes to greet
and honor him."

[HERCULES *thinks.*]

They're waiting.

HERCULES:
Very well then.

[*He rises and departs, holding the pitcher.*]

ATHENA:
Farewell, Hercules.

AMYCUS THE BOXER

[*Music for the transition, as the* ARGONAUTS *come ashore in a new land.*]

JASON:
Shipmates, what land is this, do you suppose?

POLLUX:
Whatever it is, let's go ahead and make our
fires. It's cold.

JASON:
I agree. Come, let's several of us go to gather wood.
Others stay here, tend to the ship and camp.

[DYMAS *staggers on, scared out of his wits.*]

DYMAS:
Whoever you are, get out! Go, while you still can!

JASON:
Why, what's the matter?

DYMAS [*desperate*]:
This is a dreadful place you've come to,
where the rite of guest and host is not respected. Go!
And take me with you!

JASON:
But what's the matter? Who is the ruler here?

DYMAS:
The king is Amycus, and he hates sailors,
says they are all cowards—afraid to box with him!

ARGONAUTS [*scoffing, severally*]:
We're not afraid to fight!

DYMAS [*frantically*]:
You don't know what you're saying! He's a brute!
He'll taunt you into boxing to the death, which is what he wants—
to watch your brains spill out. He killed my companion!
No one can pass by without taking up the challenge!
Turn around, and take me with you far from here!

JASON:
What is your name? Is this your home?

DYMAS:
The gods forbid! My name is Dymas:
I shipwrecked here with my companion. After
Amycus knocked his eyes from his broken head he
dismembered him—cast his parts around the shore
and then dismissed me as not worthy of a hero's death.

POLLUX [*calling out*]:
Whoever you are who did this terrible deed,
if you have limbs, then you too can be dismembered!

[AMYCUS, *a giant, approaches in the distance. The* ARGONAUTS *do not
see him, but then some notice the ground is shaking beneath their
feet with his every step.*]

DYMAS:
Stop it!—

POLLUX:
And if there is blood in your veins then you too can bleed!

JASON:
Pollux—

DYMAS:
Stop it! Are you crazy!

JASON [*noticing something*]:
Pollux, be quiet a mo—

POLLUX:
It's not for nothing I have trained my ass off all these years!
Not for nothing my coaches and my sparring partners—

JASON [*seeing* AMYCUS]:
Pollux!—

[AMYCUS *arrives. Everyone yells and scatters. He is slow-witted,
punch-drunk but lethal.*]

AMYCUS:
Hello, fools and madmen! What lured you here?
No doubt it was the stories you've heard of how we welcome
    foreigners!
I am Poseidon's son, and no one creeps along this coast without
    answering my challenge.
So far only one has survived the contest: myself, of course! Hah
    hah hah!

[*He runs around gloating and terrifying the* ARGONAUTS.]

It is my father's charge to keep these waters free of trash!

POLLUX:
Trash!? TRASH!?

CASTOR [*trying to hold him back*]:
Brother, this is no sporting match like at home
with referees and rounds!

AMYCUS:
Are you my volunteer?

POLLUX:
I'll fight any man who says I am not—as well as you!

AMYCUS:
Not much to you!

JASON:
Back off! His father's Zeus!

AMYCUS:
And mine's Poseidon.

JASON:
Athena is our guide! She built our mast!

AMYCUS:
That little girl with the crinkly red skirt? That's all you've got?
Let the contest begin! I'll smash that pretty face. Let's go!

[*He winds up and swings his massive fist but hits the mast instead
of* POLLUX. *The fight continues. Total chaos. Just as* AMYCUS *seems to
have decisively gained the upper hand, everything—shouting as*

well as action—slows down to very slow motion as POLLUX *manages to land a devastating blow, and* AMYCUS *crumples.*]

POLLUX [*speaking in "slow motion"*]:
Go to hell! And tell all the shades who greet you
it was Pollux sent you there!

ALL [*as normal motion and sound are restored*]:
Yay Pollux! Yes yes! Rah! Rah!
Pol-lux! Pol-lux! Pol-lux!

[*The* ARGONAUTS *carry* POLLUX *off on their shoulders, chanting his name.* AMYCUS *disassembles into the two people playing him. They sadly trail off, leaving* JASON *and* DYMAS *alone.*]

JASON:
Dymas, you say you are not from here?

DYMAS:
No, sir, from farther north. And you?

JASON:
We are the Argonauts, headed to Colchis.

DYMAS:
Why are you going there?

JASON:
We seek the Golden Fleece, to bring it back to its rightful homeland.

DYMAS:
Oh sir, I thank you for this rescue, and see the skill
of your crew, but you will never get that Fleece.

JASON:
Why not?

DYMAS:
First, Aeëtes is a tyrant—arrogant and hateful—and
he believes the Fleece is the source of his power.
Second—and this is worse—it's guarded by a dragon
that never sleeps.

JASON [*after a pause*]:
                              Dymas, do me this service:
don't mention these things to the crew.

DYMAS:
Sir, for you I am willing to go with you
to Colchis, and help you in whatever way I can.

HARPIES

[*A bit of music.* JASON *and* DYMAS *board the* Argo. *Other* ARGONAUTS
are at their rowing positions. Time has passed.]

JASON:
Tell me, what island is that ahead? What might we expect?

DYMAS:
Sir, I believe this is the home of Phineus.

[PHINEUS *appears in the distance, feeble and crawling. He carries a
plate of food in his shaking hand. The* ARGONAUTS *do not see him.*]

IDMON [*overhearing*]:
Phineus?

JASON:
Who is he?

IDMON:
A great prophet—alas for him!

JASON:
Why alas?

IDMON:
Zeus decided long ago that mortals should not
know all that was in store for them—so that they
would continue to make sacrifice and pray to him,
hoping for the best, not knowing what lay ahead.
Phineus told too much.

JASON:
What has Zeus done?

[PHINEUS *starts to bring some food to his mouth.*]

DYMAS:
Condemned him to live forever, but only barely.
Each time he tries to eat he is prevented.

JASON:
How prevented?

[*Harpies fly in from all sides. They harass* PHINEUS, *steal his food,
and vomit and poop on him. They fly off, cackling.*]

IDMON:

Those Harpies tear the food from his hands
and foul any that remains.

DYMAS:

                      He's skin and bones,
two hundred years old and more, but a great prophet
nonetheless.

JASON:

Pull into harbor there! I wish to make inquiries
of this Phineus. Are the Harpies dangerous?

[JASON, DYMAS, ATALANTA, *and* IDMON *are now walking onshore.*]

DYMAS:

Only to him, I think. Yet they are so foul,
it can be difficult to breathe when they're around.

IDMON [*catching a whiff of* PHINEUS]:
Oh Zeus!

PHINEUS:

Can it be? Can it be? Are you the Argonauts come at last?

JASON:

Sir, we are.

[JASON *tries to be polite and not recoil as* PHINEUS *crawls toward him and clings to him. The others cover their mouths and noses.*]

PHINEUS:

Please don't sail away! Don't abandon me,
but save me—for so it has been foretold.
You have onboard a son of Boreas, is it not so?

JASON:

Yes—Zetes. Atalanta, run quick and fetch him—
and bring some food as well.

PHINEUS:

He has the power of flight?

JASON:

He does. Listen, if we are able to save you from the Harpies,
tell me—will you answer truthfully our questions
about our voyage?

PHINEUS:

                      Gladly, I will tell you all,
only there may not be much time, for I believe
when the Harpies leave, my life will leave me too.

JASON [*as* ATALANTA *returns*]:
Here is Atalanta with some food.

PHINEUS:

And here come the Harpies too!

[*The Harpies come in, circling and harassing the* ARGONAUTS *and* PHINEUS. ZETES *enters.*]

JASON:
Chase them, Zetes! Chase them far away!

[ZETES *chases the Harpies away.*]

They've fallen in the sea!

PHINEUS [*desperate, famished*]:
Bread! Bread!

JASON:
                    Quick! What lies ahead?

[JASON *pushes bread into* PHINEUS's *mouth, making* PHINEUS *hard to understand. He repeats* PHINEUS's *lines as necessary.*]

PHINEUS:
Before the land of Colchis you must pass
the crashing rocks—destroyers of ships, mountains
that come together and then pull back.

JASON:
Go on!

PHINEUS:
Send a bird through the passage first,
then as the stones pull back, drive with
all your might through the channel.

JASON:
What next?

PHINEUS:
There is betrayal in your future, Jason,
one which will benefit you and one—

[PHINEUS *is dying.*]

JASON:
How shall I win the Golden Fleece?

PHINEUS:
Look . . . to the corner . . . of the room.
Fare . . . well.

[PHINEUS *dies.*]

JASON:
Look to the corner of the room?

CLASHING ROCKS

[*All the* ARGONAUTS *take up their rowing positions. They are overcome by dread. Ominous sound.*]

ATHENA:
They haul the anchor stone and set out once
again, rowing fearfully, reluctantly, for now they know
what lies ahead. They peer out to port and starboard.

CASTOR:
Which side are they on?

ATHENA:
The waves begin to swell.

UNCLE:
The sea is churning.

IDMON:
We're losing two yards for every yard we row!

[ATHENA *holds two small stones in her hands. She slams them together and pulls them apart throughout the scene.* HERA *enters dragging a little replica of the* Argo *on a string. There is the enormous booming sound of the clashing rocks, wind, and churning sea.*]

ATHENA:
They hear them before they see them: two
enormous jagged mountains, pulling apart
and slamming back together, sending up
a spume of sea spray high as the cliff's summit.

[*The* ARGONAUTS *abandon their posts, shouting and clinging to the mast in terror.*]

ARGONAUTS [*variously*]:
We'll never make it! They'll crush us all!
It isn't possible! We haven't the strength!

[JASON *pulls them off the mast, driving them to their positions.*]

JASON:
Shipmates, panic drives the gods away from men!
Keep your wits about you! We were afraid at

Amycus's island, but we did not show our terror!
Back to your oars, men, and row!
The gods will aid our valor!

TIPHYS:
Men, ready at your oars!
Euphemos! Release the bird, let her go!

[EUPHEMOS *releases a bird. Slowly it arcs over their heads and away.
At the same time,* HERA *manipulates a tiny replica of the bird moving between the stones in* ATHENA's *hands.*]

TIPHYS:
She's made it through! Now pull, men, pull. Bend your oars!
Faster! Faster!

JASON:
Athena, Goddess, help us!

[*With enormous effort,* ATHENA *holds the stones apart.* HERA *pulls
the little boat through* ATHENA's *legs.*]

ARGONAUTS:
We're through! We're through!

[*They drop their oars in exhaustion.*]

ATHENA:
The ship rounds a final point, and suddenly,
rising before them
is the forbidding palace of Aeëtes, king of Colchis.
The sun emerges from the clouds for a moment

and catches on something hung on a barren tree. It shines out: the glittering Golden Fleece.

[*Thunder. A flash of light catches the Golden Fleece.*]

ACT II

SCHEMES

[*The rigging raised on the* Argo *during the launch is now down. The Golden Fleece is no longer visible.* HERA *and* ATHENA *sit.* ATHENA *is sharpening her spear with a stone.*]

HERA:
Daughter of Zeus, what's to be done?
How shall we help our Argonauts
now that they have come so far—to the very shores of Colchis?
Have you thought of any trick to help them
get that Golden Fleece and take it back to Hellas?

ATHENA:
I've been weighing various plans, but nothing is quite right.

HERA:
It seems unlikely they'll be able to sweet-talk Aeëtes
into surrendering the Fleece as he should, he's so appallingly arrogant.

ATHENA:
He's impossible.

HERA:
But clever. I don't think our Argonauts can deceive him.

ATHENA:
No. Not on their own. Nor are their numbers great
enough to take his army on in battle—brave and skilled
though they are.

HERA:
Hmm.

[*A pause.* ATHENA *continues to sharpen her spear.*]

Wait—

ATHENA:
What is it?

HERA:
He has a daughter, doesn't he? What's her name—?

ATHENA [*uninterested*]:
Medea.

HERA:
What do you know of her?

ATHENA:
She's a drug-wise girl. She busies herself all day with
spells and charms, gathering the herbs and oils

of the fields and forests, mixing them up in secret ways.
Although young—a maiden still—she's able to call up storms,
I hear, and soothe them, and she has birds and animals
at her command—but what use is she to us? Another weapon
in her father's armory.

HERA:
No, listen, listen: let's go call on Aphrodite.

ATHENA:
Aphrodite? That little bit of fluff? No one could be more useless!

HERA:
No. I have a plan. Come along and don't offend her. Let's go.

APHRODITE

[ATHENA *and* HERA *fly through the air. They land suddenly in the home of* APHRODITE, *who sits looking at herself in a mirror, having her hair combed, and being fanned by servants. Harp music plays.*]

APHRODITE [*startled*]:
Dear ladies! To what do I owe this honor?
Come in, sit down, please.

HERA:
Why, thank you.

APHRODITE:
Refresh yourselves.

HERA:
We will.

[*During the following the servants go off and return variously with wine and seats for the goddesses.* HERA *sits and drinks, but* ATHENA *declines the wine and scrapes her sandal on the upholstery, then stands with one foot on the seat, her forearm on her knee.*]

APHRODITE:
I must confess I'm startled. Hitherto, I've not received
many visits from you—high goddesses as you are,
I'm surprised you could find the house.

HERA:
                                        Very witty, I'm sure.

[HERA *waves her hand to stop the annoying harp music.*]

But what concerns us is a serious problem. Even now
Jason and his crew are outside Aeëtes's palace at Colchis
wondering how they will lay their hands upon the Golden Fleece.
Jason, were he to venture to the underworld itself, I would protect,
for he carried me once across a river when I was disguised—as an
    old woman!—
to test men's righteousness. Now his fate is in your hands, our dear
    friend,
it is up to you to save him.

APHRODITE:
                            What are you saying?
Reverend Goddess, I can't go to war!

[APHRODITE *makes a face and shudders.*]
92

ATHENA:
Ha!

APHRODITE:
I am honored, but—

[*She looks at her nails.*]

eeeew.

HERA [*more diplomatically*]:
No, no. We're not asking you to fight.
All you need do is get that boy of yours to charm Aeëtes's daughter,
Medea—to aim one of his shafts at that spell-soaked girl.
If the arrow hits her right, she will do anything for him, and
she must know the secrets of the Fleece
and her father's mind and ways.

APHRODITE:
Get my boy—? You think that's easy? There's no
controlling that one, no commanding him! He does
what he wants when he wants. No one is safe
when he's around! And besides, Athena, Hera, you'd
have better luck with him than I. He treats me with contempt,
he cares nothing for me, always provokes me—
and indeed plagued with his naughtiness, I've been minded
to smash up his bow and nasty-sounding arrows—
in public! The threats he utters when he is angry!

[ATHENA *and* HERA *have difficulty disguising their amusement at this.*]

Oh yes! Others find my troubles a joke.

HERA:
Won't you at least try, dear friend?

[HERA *approaches her.* ATHENA *lowers her spear in* APHRODITE'S
direction.]

APHRODITE:
Well, as this is a plan that you both cherish I'll do my best
to coax him: perhaps since it's mischief
you have in mind he'll do it.

HERA:
Thank you, Aphrodite. We won't forget this.

[HERA *and* ATHENA *begin their exit.*]

APHRODITE:
Yes, all right. Farewell.

[*As soon as they are across* APHRODITE'S *threshold, they laugh and
congratulate each other.* ATHENA *is impressed.*]

ATHENA:
I never could have thought of such a thing!
My father bore me to know nothing of such pangs—
all that longing and madness! Ugh.
I've never felt the smallest need to charm a man's desires,
and I've never understood it in gods or men.
But I'll believe you that this could work, for I've seen
what love has done to others, though he has never
done a thing to me. Let's go!

[*They fly off.* APHRODITE, *left behind in her home, has been looking around. She calls her son.*]

APHRODITE:
Eros! Eros! Where are you? Come here! Eros!

[*He flies in from above. He's been eating chocolate cake, or is pulling gum out of his mouth—some sign of mischief. He hangs midair throughout the following.*]

EROS:
What's up?

APHRODITE:
What are you grinning at, you unspeakable little horror?
What have you been up to?

[*He cackles.*]

Oh, never mind.
Listen now: if you're willing to do the job I tell you—

EROS:
What'll I get?

APHRODITE:
                              I'm telling you!
I'll give you one of Zeus's most beautiful playthings—
you'll never find a better toy.

EROS:
Ha!

APHRODITE:
A well-rounded ball, its rings are fashioned of gold,
all the way round, and its seams are hidden with
spirals of cobalt.

EROS [*considering*]:
Huh.

APHRODITE:
Anytime you toss this ball
it unleashes a gleaming, airy trail of sparks like a meteor.
This I shall give you—if you will shoot Aeëtes's virgin
daughter full of desire for Jason.

EROS:
You promise?

APHRODITE:
And do it soon.

EROS:
You promise? No one's more deceitful than you!

APHRODITE:
Your dearest head, and my own, now be my witness
that, yes, I'll give you this present, I won't cheat you,
so long as you put a shaft into Aeëtes's daughter.

[EROS *flies off.*]

AEËTES

[*Brief music. Drums. The palace of Aeëtes.* AEËTES'S SERVANT *enters with* JASON, IDMON, *and* CASTOR *following.* CASTOR *is carrying an olive branch.*]

AEËTES'S SERVANT:
Wait here.

[*He departs.*]

CASTOR:
Jason, are you sure that this is right?
To come here unarmed and simply ask?

JASON:
It is, my friend, I'm sure of it. We have
come safely to this palace which
others declared beyond the ends of the earth.
Our dangers now are passed. My guess is he'll simply
say yes and give us what we're asking. But
if he should refuse us or insult us and send us away,
don't be disheartened, we're not leaving without the Fleece.

[AEËTES *has entered on the bridge above.* AEËTES'S SERVANT *has entered below, carrying a chair that he places in a corner. A young girl,* MEDEA, *follows and sits in the chair, unnoticed by all. She wears a simple white dress. Her arms and legs are tattooed with signs and runes. When* AEËTES *speaks, he never raises his voice. He is cunning, arrogant, even elegant.*]

AEËTES:

And who are you? You belong to that vessel,
I suppose, that I see in my harbor?

JASON:

Sire, Hyperion's son, the gods have brought me here.
I have come in the first ship to cross the vast breadth of the seas.
I come, as Phrixus did, from Greece, but I am not here
to seek revenge. Nor have I fled my homeland as Phrixus did.
And yet it was not my own idea to make this journey.
King Pelias of Thessaly commanded me to come.
Kings can be cruel, and their subjects must somehow endure.
The charge my uncle gave me was to journey here to fetch
the Fleece of the golden ram that carried Phrixus to your door.
I do as I am bidden—and find myself your supplicant.
Do not begrudge the Argonauts the glory of the gift we ask:
it is only right.

AEËTES:

                    What a pretty speech.
Had you not already crossed my threshold
carrying the olive branch I would cut out your tongues
and chop off your hands—yes both of them—and send you on
     your way
furnished with feet alone as recompense for your lies
about the blessed gods. Get out of here, sea trash!
It's not the Fleece you want, it is my land. My crown.

JASON:
Sire—

AEËTES:

Who is this Pelias you speak of? Thessaly? Where is that?
A boat lands with fifty outlaws and demands of me,
a sovereign king, part of my national treasure?
Why not our precious gold? Why not our daughters?

JASON:

Sire, we mean you no harm—

AEËTES:

Where you come from, do you have parents?
Families? Homes, perhaps? Or are you a band of brigands,
savages who roam the earth living on what you plunder?

JASON:

I swear; it was heaven that drove me here, and the
cold-blooded fiat of a king.

AEËTES:

Outlaws, I shouldn't wonder, and exiles your king
has forbidden to come home ever—except with that Fleece,
a bribe he might accept. But before I give that up,
those mountains will come down here with their forests felled
to dance on the shore and swim in the sea like dolphins
in the wake of your Greek ship.

JASON:

                    Sire, we are prepared
to compensate you for the Fleece, with gifts or
service, whatever you demand. Our ship is
filled with men of extraordinary skill,
great strength, and prophecy, the ability to—

AEËTES:
Oh, you needn't bore me with the endless details
about your stinking crew.
I'll make you an offer—take it or leave it:
I have here, out at pasture on the plain of Ares,
two brazen-footed bulls, who snort fire.
Yoke those beasts, as I can, and make them plow
the field, and in each furrow plant not Demeter's corn seed
but the teeth of a terrible serpent. If you can do this,
the Fleece is yours.

IDMON [urgently to JASON]:
He's crazy. Let's get out of here.

JASON:
Aeëtes, it is your right to press me on this matter,
so this ordeal of yours, outrageous as it is,
I shall dare. Believe it, I shall.

AEËTES:
Go back to your company then, if you're so hot for hard work.
We'll see you on the plain in two days' time,
but if your nerve cracks and you fail,
I shall have the right to make of your crew an example
to any other foreigner who'd trouble me,
and burn them up in the hull of that ship of yours.

[AEËTES exits. APHRODITE and EROS enter, unseen. EROS aims his
arrow toward MEDEA.]

CASTOR:
It's impossible!

JASON:
Never mind, we'll find a way.

[JASON *starts to go, but* IDMON *stops him.*]

IDMON:
Jason, look into the corner of the room.

EROS [*whispering*]:
Medea!

IDMON:
Do you see something?

EROS:
Medea!

[*Music: a long sustained note. The following may take as long as thirty seconds. Everything slows down. As* JASON *turns to look in all four corners of the room,* EROS *lets fly his arrow.* APHRODITE *carries the arrow toward* MEDEA *very slowly, as* MEDEA *turns to look toward* EROS *and starts to stand.* APHRODITE *plunges the arrow into* MEDEA*'s heart. The normal pace of life returns.* MEDEA *runs from the room.* APHRODITE *tosses a small ball to* EROS *and they both exit.*]

JASON:
There was only a girl there, she's gone now.

[JASON, IDMON, *and* CASTOR *begin to walk through the hallways of the palace rapidly.* JASON *is in a rage.*]

CASTOR:
What do we do? Do we take the ship now and flee?

JASON:

That isn't possible, you know it's not. We can't
have come all this way for nothing. That's what Pelias wants,
and Aeëtes as well, both of them, to watch us fail,
and to see shame settle forever upon all of our heads.

CASTOR:

But how can you undertake this task?

JASON:

I'll find a way. Oh! This pair of tyrants!
Are they in league with one another?
We cross an ocean to find an ocean of trouble!

IDMON:

Do we tell the crew what happened?

JASON:

Of course, this is all our trial.

IDMON:

They'll despair.

JASON:

You're underestimating them. They'll bear up.

[JASON, IDMON, *and* CASTOR *exit.*]

MEDEA

[*Music: low, pulsing, and ominous.* MEDEA *enters. There is an arrow
through her heart, its shaft visible on both sides of her body. Her*

white dress is stained with blood around the wound. She is giddy, astonished, rapidly moving from girlish laughter to weeping and back again.]

MEDEA:
What is happening? What has happened?
That man—that Jason! How he braved my father—
and how he looked while he was doing it!
I've never seen such a thing: the way he stood
and spoke so beautifully—
the way his eyes flashed when he said,
"Believe me, I shall . . ." His voice!
What if he had come, not to bear the Fleece away,
but me? What if it were I that was his heart's desire?

What am I thinking? I'll never see him again.
He's bound to sail away again to Greece—
or else he's sure to die: only Father can yoke those bulls—
and then the serpent's teeth—!
O Gods, protect him! Let him not perish!
Or if he must, let him know that I took no part in it.
No—nor any joy either. Oh, let him be safe!

[*The music shifts. During the following,* THREE MEN *enter. On the words, "She went to bed,"* MEDEA *falls back into their arms as they lift her in the air. Slowly she twists and turns, now rising above their heads, now falling in their arms, in constant, slow, even motion.*]

ATHENA:
So Medea spoke to herself for many hours,
playing the scene over and over again in her mind
as Love the destroyer burned in her heart.
She went to bed, but Love kept sleep at bay;

she tossed and turned all night,
as desire flooded every part of her.
Like those gentle southern breezes
which begin by tousling the topmost boughs of trees
but then suddenly turn strong to buffet the helpless ships at sea,
so love first shimmered on Medea, then bore her down.

[*Music ends.* MEDEA *lies on the ground. The* MEN *depart.*]

BACK AT CAMP

[MEDEA *remains sleeping.* JASON, IDMON, DYMAS, UNCLE, TIPHYS, *and*
MELEAGER *enter. They open the trapdoor and firelight shines up, il-*
luminating them from below. MELEAGER *sits apart.* ATHENA *watches*
and listens above.]

TIPHYS:
Jason, no one will blame you if we abandon
this adventure. Aeëtes is at fault. It will have been
enough we made the journey and traveled safely home.

JASON:
No, I am determined.

TIPHYS:
But what can you do alone against those bulls?

IDMON:
Jason, think again, what was in the corners of the room
when we spoke to Aeëtes? Did you look in all four?

JASON:

Yes, and I tell you there was nothing—no weapon,
no treasure—nothing. Just that young girl.

DYMAS:

A girl?

JASON:

Yes.

DYMAS:

Aeëtes's daughter?

JASON:

She could be I suppose. She entered when he did, I think.

DYMAS:

If it was his daughter, she's no ordinary girl, believe me.
She's a sort of witch who studies all kinds of spells and charms.

JASON:

Her? I can't believe it. This girl was modest, she never
looked up, except for once. A maiden, surely.

DYMAS:

That's her! Medea! Her father always keeps her near.
They say she can summon storms, or stop the moon
in its tracks, charm animals—all sorts of things.

JASON:

Truly?

DYMAS:
Circe is her aunt.

IDMON:
Circe herself?

DYMAS:
Yes.

IDMON:
This girl is our salvation, Jason, I am sure of it.

MELEAGER [*emerging from the shadows*]:
What? You want to pin the hopes of our success
on the witchcraft of a maid? Not on our own skill? Our valor?

UNCLE:
Stop it, Meleager.

IDMON [*to* JASON]:
Phineus himself directed your gaze into that corner.
We must look to her, I'm certain of it.

JASON:
But if she is the daughter of Aeëtes, how shall I win her over?
How even meet her?

DYMAS:
She is a devotee of Hecate, who has a temple here.

IDMON:
Tomorrow is the full moon—she's bound to be attending then.
Go there tomorrow night, Jason. Slip through the woods
and find her, plead your cause.

MELEAGER:
Tomorrow night you should be sleeping,
preparing for the battle with those bulls.

IDMON:
Do as I say, Jason.

[*The* ARGONAUTS *and* HYLAS *depart.*]

CIRCE

[HERA *enters, wearing a sorceress's robe.*]

ATHENA:
Everything's going well.

HERA:
Indeed.

ATHENA:
Nice disguise.

HERA:
Thank you.

ATHENA:
Don't you trust the strength of that boy's arrows?
Or do you just like dressing up?

HERA:
A little push can't hurt.

ATHENA:
Very well.

[HERA *steps into* MEDEA's *room.*]

HERA:
Medea?

MEDEA [*waking*]:
Aunt Circe? Is it really you?

ATHENA:
No.

HERA [*as* CIRCE]:
How beautiful you are! How you've grown!

MEDEA:
What are you doing here? It's been years.
Did you bring your marvelous team of serpents?

[MEDEA *begins to run to the window.* HERA *stops her.*]

HERA [*as* CIRCE]:
They're just outside.

MEDEA:

Is it because you learned the Greeks have come,
all the way across the ocean, braving all to see our land?
Did that remind you of Colchis and all its marvels?

[MEDEA *fetches a seat for* HERA, *then kneels beside her.*]

HERA [*as* CIRCE]:

Why, darling niece, you alone are the cause of my visit.

MEDEA:

I?

HERA [*as* CIRCE]:

You are no longer a child, Medea, you must marry soon,
and I've come to see, who are your suitors?
Who has my brother chosen for you? He has so
little judgment in such things.

MEDEA:

That's just it, Aunt! My father has engaged me to Styrus, a man
for whom I feel absolutely nothing. Meanwhile—
you've come just in time! Something has
gone wrong with me: Sleep never comes to me anymore,
I'm troubled all the time in mind and spirit. I can't eat:
I feel as though I am burning up in . . . and then sometimes
I am so cold I shiver. Surely you must know a cure?

HERA [*as* CIRCE]:

Is it not time for you yourself to begin to practice in earnest
the spells and charms and potions you have been readying
all your life?

MEDEA:
Well . . .

HERA [*as* CIRCE]:
Listen, I'll tell you a curious tale of something I saw
as I landed. There is a glorious ship in the harbor.

MEDEA:
That's them! That's the Greeks!

HERA [*as* CIRCE]:
Truly a marvel—

MEDEA:
Yes!

HERA [*as* CIRCE]:
And its crew are all handsome men, but their leader,
their captain and prince, is the best looking of all—

MEDEA:
That's Jason! Jason!

HERA [*as* CIRCE]:
Well, seeing me approach the palace and thinking,
I suppose, that I might know you, he came up to me and said:
"Lady, as one who is fated soon to die, I beg you
do me a service and take this word to the ear of your young mistress."

MEDEA:
To me? He said that?

110

HERA [*as* CIRCE]:
"Say I pray to her image alone. Athena and Hera have failed me,
and she is my last remaining hope. If she were to save me
from a cruel death I would be hers, body and soul."

MEDEA:
Oh!

HERA [*as* CIRCE]:
And here he broke off and drew his sword, as if he would fall
on the naked blade—

MEDEA:
Oh no!

HERA [*as* CIRCE]:
But I stopped his hand and promised.

MEDEA:
To tell me this?

HERA [*as* CIRCE]:
Yes. Oh, he was so desperate, I am tempted to help him myself,
but it was to you, Medea, that he addressed himself.
I have done enough to establish the reputation of my powers,
now is your chance to do the same. This is the moment of your life,
Medea; will you not aid the noble stranger?
Go tonight to Hecate's temple. Meet him there.

MEDEA:
But Aunt . . . how can I manage? And my father,
my brothers—

HERA [*as* CIRCE]:
You'll find a way, Medea. You'll find a way.

[HERA *exits.*]

MEDEA:
Alas! What shall I do?

[*She takes the arrow by both hands and tries to pull it out, but it will not budge.*]

There is no remedy for this pain of mine!
How can I betray my father? How can I not?
No: let the contest destroy him, if that is his destiny!
Oh no, no. He must not die. He must not die.
What shall I do? O Gods, what shall I do?
Why did they come? What will my kinsmen say:
"This girl, helpless in the face of her dirty lust for a Greek,
shaming her parents, her country, and herself."
They'll say that forever.
No. Better to end it here,
in this room. Tonight.

[*Music.*]

ATHENA:
Poor girl. She went to a hidden place
where she kept a little casket.

[MEDEA *searches through her casket, unstops a little bottle, and raises it to her lips. One of the doors opens.*]

But then, all of a sudden,
she saw the door of Hades open. She saw the dark.
And at that moment, behind her, through the window the dawn
began to break and a voice within her said,
[*whispering*] "Medea, look at the sun."

She remembered all the
many delights that exist among the living,
she thought of her happy companions, as young girls will,
and the sun grew sweeter to look at than ever before.

[MEDEA *lowers the poison. Music shifts.* MEDEA *returns the poison to the casket and retrieves another vial as well as a small stone.*]

BY MOONLIGHT

[APHRODITE, *carrying a bucket, enters from one door and pulls* MEDEA *along into the woods. At the same time,* HERA *enters from the other door and pushes* JASON *along his path until the two are standing opposite at some distance from each other. They are left alone, the bucket at* MEDEA'S *feet. Music ends. A pause.* MEDEA *is terrified.* JASON *is struck by her beauty, her youth, and although he has come with the purpose of pleading and perhaps seducing, he also falls in love. During the following, he slowly, carefully approaches* MEDEA *until he is kneeling at her feet.*]

JASON:
Sweet girl, don't turn away. Don't be afraid.
It is true, I have sought you out alone, but
I'm not like those other loudmouthed braggarts
you'll find around, I'll not speak of this. Now tell me.

Do you look at me with pity or with scorn?
Will it please you to watch the poor foreigner die?
I will not refuse to undertake what your father commands,
just as I will not leave this place alive without the Fleece.
So tell me, could so lovely a face mask a savage heart? Dear girl,
I come to you as guest and suppliant, kneeling before you
in my need: my life and those of many kings
are held in your small hands—

[*He tries to take her hands. She pulls away, highly agitated.*]

MEDEA:
Do you know what you are asking me?
These trees that thought they knew me are wondering,
"Is this Aeëtes's daughter? Is this Medea?"
I am a stranger even to myself. What am I doing here?

JASON:
You are here to save me.

MEDEA [*sinking to the ground*]:
Why ever did you leave your home and come to trouble us?
For glory? To right an ancient wrong?
Did you think we would throw flowers at your feet?
Welcome the invading foreigners?

JASON:
I know I have no right—

MEDEA:
They say you are loved by Hera herself, and Athena
is your guide. Where are they now?

114

JASON [*touching her face, gently*]:
They left me to a native princess.

MEDEA [*clasping his hands*]:
Please tell me: if there is still a chance
those goddesses may help you, or if your own strength
is enough for these ordeals, I beg you, send me home.
Pity me. Send me home before I do what I am about to do.

[*They are very close.*]

JASON:
I look to you alone, dear girl. Your skill, your faith, your power
alone will save me and the crew. Through you our mothers
and fathers who are even now lamenting on the shore
will see their sorrow cast to the winds, as we return,
giving praise and glory to your name, Medea. Our gratitude
and that of the gods will live forever.

MEDEA [*revealing the vial*]:
Here: with this I give you myself, my name, my honor.
And if I could draw the soul from my body
and give you that, I would.

[*She hands him the vial. He begins to kiss her. She pulls away.*]

                         Here is what we must do.
Mix this in with the water from Hecate's spring, and
rub it on yourself like oil. Within it are great strength
and great protection too. But you'll not stay immune
for long. By this time tomorrow night it will be
gone. Yet for one day, nothing can harm you.

JASON:
Are you certain—

MEDEA:
Yes. Do it now! We have no time to lose!

JASON:
Now?

MEDEA:
Yes!

[*She turns her back.* JASON *pours the vial into the water in the bucket. He takes a cloth from the bucket, takes off his tunic, and begins to wash himself. Time passes. The only sound is that of the water, his washing, and* MEDEA's *breathing as she tries not to watch. He turns and holds out his cloth to her.*]

JASON:
Will you help?

[*She takes the cloth and washes his back in silence for several moments then turns away.*]

MEDEA:
There's something else you ought to know. When
you sow those serpents' teeth, that's not the end.
Warriors will spring up from the field. When they
attack, take this stone, once held by Discord herself,
and throw it amid them. They will turn against each other.

JASON:
Your name will live forever, Medea.

[*They kiss. Then she pulls away.*]

MEDEA:
                              No more.
Only, tell me what part of the sky to look to when you're gone,
what star to guide my gaze toward your native land.
There I'll fix my eyes each night till I grow old—
and if my father finds what I have done,
I'll turn my eyes there as I die, and rejoice
that sometimes Jason still recalls the night
he knelt by me and was not ashamed
to be saved by the skill of a girl.

JASON [*embracing her*]:
                              Daughter of Aeëtes,
do you think I could accept your help and then abandon you?
If so, then remove your spells and send me to my death.
What love of life could I maintain with such shame upon me?
I will see you in the port at home, and watch the people come
to stare in wonder as you approach in your glittering Golden Fleece.

MEDEA:
Can this be true?

JASON:
I swear,

[*The sound of scratching. Unseen by the lovers, a winged* FURY *enters slowly, writing down what* JASON *says.* MEDEA *grows giddy, laughing and kissing* JASON *as the oath goes on.*]

if I ever forget this night, what you have done to
save my life, your flight from your father and your home,
then let my triumph over the bulls
and the soldiers that spring from the earth and the Fleece itself
be worthless and hateful to me.
Let your magic turn against me in our own home,
let me be terrified, and let no one be near to help me;
and if you can think of more dreadful things to do,
add them, for I shall have deserved the worst that you can do
as you turn away from me.

MEDEA [*laughing, teasingly putting a finger to his lips*]:
Careful! Or a Fury who records the vows of lovers
may hear you and hold you to it.

JASON:
The gods grant one does.

[*The* FURY *cackles and exits. Drumming.* JASON *and* MEDEA *run off.*]

BULLS

[AEËTES *enters above. All the* ARGONAUTS *except* JASON *enter and
stand on the periphery. The closed doors shake and rattle as though
being struck by the ferocious beasts behind them.*]

IDMON [*with* MELEAGER *beside him*]:
My leader is waiting on the field of Ares,
impatient to meet your bronze-footed bulls to try
his strength.

AEËTES:
What? Still here?
Challenging me? Then let the bulls be brought out
and we'll see if he can yoke them, withstand their fiery breath,
and plow the field with them.

[*Aside*] And then, when the crop comes in, we'll watch as the impudent
Greek harvests what he has planted. How splendid to
see foreigners die in sight of the Fleece, and perhaps decorate
with their gushing blood the prize they fail to take.

[JASON *enters holding the yoke, with a satchel of serpents' teeth across his shoulder. Music and loud drumming.* MEDEA *enters above near her father. The red stain on her dress is significantly larger. The* BULLS *enter. They storm toward* JASON. *He is thrown to the ground, but* MEDEA *begins to cast her spell. The* BULLS *are entranced and submit to being yoked.* JASON *drives them off, casting the serpents' teeth as he goes. He returns triumphant.* MEDEA *collapses from her effort. The drumming momentarily slows and subsides.*]

JASON:
What do you think of that, Aeëtes! [*To* IDMON] Give me a drink of water!

AEËTES:
Just wait a moment, Jason, wait a moment.
Your crop is coming in.

[SKELETON SOLDIERS *appear from the earth. They approach and begin to attack* JASON; *he is almost driven mad with terror and confusion.*]

MEDEA:
The stone, Jason—the stone!

[JASON *recovers himself and throws the stone among the* SKELETON SOLDIERS. *They break apart and disappear. The ordeal of music and drumming is over. The* ARGONAUTS *rush in, cheering and congratulating* JASON.]

ESCAPE AND DRAGON

[AEËTES *is enraged. He notices* MEDEA *by his side.*]

AEËTES:
Is this your doing?

MEDEA:
Jason!

[*She begins to run.*]

AEËTES:
Is this your doing?

MEDEA [*shouting to* JASON]:
Follow me! He'll never give you the Fleece, never!
Back to the temple!

JASON [*to the* ARGONAUTS]:
Back to the ship! Prepare to fly! I'll meet you there.

[JASON *runs off with* MEDEA *as the* ARGONAUTS *run the other way. The scene continues.*]

AEËTES:
Styrus! Apsyrtos!

[STYRUS, *Medea's fiancé, and* APSYRTOS, *her brother, enter.*]

Tell me, Styrus, does it make you happy to see your betrothed
running off with a Greek? Apsyrtos, are you thrilled your sister
is a whore? Dishonoring all of us? Shaming us,
our name, and our nation forever!
She's laughing at us! Can't you hear her?
Would that I had cut out her heart when I met her in her mother's
    arms!
But it's not too late: I'll tear her limb from limb.
Gather a fleet like the world has never seen. Give chase
to those marauding sea dogs! Bring that muttering bitch back
while I devise a thousand ways to watch her die.

[*They exit variously.* MEDEA *and* JASON *run on.*]

MEDEA:
Jason, I leave my father's house, and my family's wealth,
my mother, my companions, and all the world for you.
Promise me—promise me you'll keep me forever!
Be true to your pledge and to me!

JASON:
Ah my dearest, your coming to me shall bring to me and my people
the greatest glory. In you alone, my voyage is well rewarded,
without any further prize of an animal's hide.

And yet—and yet,
I ask you to help me even further and grant that I may fulfill
the hard command that was laid upon me.
My comrades have suffered so long.

MEDEA:
The gods have heard your words, and these trees witness your vow.
Come on.

ATHENA:
They ran through the pathless woods. She knew every step, every
    branch above and every twisting root below.

[*The dragon enters.*]

JASON:
O Gods! What is it?

MEDEA:
It's him. Stay back, my love, stay back!

JASON:
How can I approach him?

MEDEA:
You mustn't. I am his mistress and he knows me well.
Now stay back, Jason.

JASON:
Maiden, I am in awe of you.

MEDEA [*to the dragon*]:
My darling, listen to me.
You may turn away from the Fleece now, close your eyes and rest.
It's been so long, has it not, since you closed your eyes?
As long as I'm here you have no reason for apprehension.
I'll guard the treasure myself, and you may relax your vigil
and at long last sleep.

[*She blows a magic powder toward him from the palm of her hand.
The dragon sleeps. But her speech has cast a spell on* JASON *as well,
and he is also asleep.*]

Jason, wake up! Quickly Jason, go! Hurry!

[JASON *runs off.* MEDEA *addresses the sleeping dragon.*]

Oh, I am sorry, poor friend. Do you remember
when I was a child and brought you
a honey cake after supper and you'd nibble it out of my hand?
What can I say? This way I didn't need to kill you.
Oh, but when you wake, you'll look at your tree and see that the
    Fleece
is gone and slink away in shame. Forget about me. Forgive me.
And do not come hissing and spitting to follow where I have gone.

JASON [*returning with the Fleece*]:
Look Medea! The Golden Fleece!

[*The dragon stirs.*]

MEDEA:
Hurry, he's waking!

ATHENA:

Off they went through the night back to the ship.

PURSUIT

[*The* ARGONAUTS *are holding their oars, waiting near the ship and peering into the dark.*]

DYMAS:

I think I see something—there! There! Can you see? I think it's him!

IDMON:

Does he have it? Does he have the Fleece?

TIPHYS:

Can you tell?

DYMAS:

Yes—I see it gleaming on his shoulders.

[*The* ARGONAUTS *cheer.*]

TIPHYS:

Wait, wait. Can that be someone with him?

MELEAGER:

Is someone pursuing him? Is he armed?

TIPHYS:

It's a girl.

IDMON:
A girl? She's with him?

MELEAGER:
He can't be serious!

TIPHYS:
Perhaps she has something she needs to tell us, or—

[JASON *and* MEDEA *run on hand in hand. Her dress is now almost entirely stained red. He is carrying the Fleece.*]

JASON:
Men, we have succeeded! The Golden Fleece!

[*Great cheering.*]

But quickly men, we must depart; I doubt
Aeëtes will be content to let us sail away
bearing both his daughter and the Fleece.

[*The* ARGONAUTS *begin to board, going up to the bridge with their oars.*]

MELEAGER:
Why are we bearing them both?

JASON [*ignoring* MELEAGER]:
Tiphys, set our course all the way back to Iolcos—quickly.

TIPHYS:
Son of Aeson, ought we not look for a different way home?
Remember those rocks that crash together are behind us.
Let's head up the river and find another passage to the sea.

JASON:

A wise suggestion, Tiphys. I accept it.
Plot a course that is perhaps longer but no doubt safer.

[*As the* ARGONAUTS *begin to row,* APSYRTOS *enters and addresses an
unseen crowd.*]

APSYRTOS:

Men of Colchis, make haste to pursue this common robber
who flees with Phrixus's sacred Fleece and the princess—my sister.
I want the lives of all those Argonauts, and their ship sunk to the
     bottom!

[*He exits.*]

TIPHYS:

Row, men, row!

[*The* ARGONAUTS *row on the bridge with all their might.* JASON *and*
MEDEA *are below.*]

JASON:

                              My darling girl,
as long as you are a maid, your father has some claim on you,
and those rulers of any lands in which we come to port may feel
     compelled
to return you to his murderous arms, because they believe it right,
or because they fear Aeëtes's wrath. I long to wed you in the sight
of my parents, in my home, with all the honors we are due. But I am
     afraid,
dear girl, we cannot wait.

MEDEA:

I do not want to wait.

JASON:

No, nor I, in truth. I cannot wait. But where shall we find
a bridal bower on this rough-hewn ship? We have only seaman's
quarters—rough hammocks and the deck itself.

MEDEA:

The chamber of my heart is room enough. And for a bed—

[*She takes the Fleece from* JASON's *shoulders and spreads it on the ground.*]

ATHENA:

Oh yes they did. Right there, on the Fleece itself.

[*Music. During the following,* MEDEA *and* JASON *embrace and make love on the Fleece. Gold falls from the sky. The rowing of the* ARGONAUTS *becomes slow, dreamy.*]

O merciless Love, great affliction, great bane to all mankind.
From you come wretched quarrels, ordeals, and lamentation,
and surging in over these, other griefs beyond counting—
but also this: the soul in the other soul for a moment,
all they know of heaven on this earth.

[*Music ends. Low drums. The rowing resumes its rapid pace.* JASON *climbs to the bridge. Throughout the following,* AEËTES, STYRUS, *and* APSYRTOS *enter below, each slowly dragging a little flotilla of minia-ture boats on long cords. They leave them surrounding the sleeping* MEDEA *and exit.*]

TIPHYS:
Row, men, row! The entire Colchian fleet is in pursuit!

MELEAGER:
Is this what we deserve, having worked so hard and suffered
and come all this way? To be slaughtered on the sea by
an alien army? Is Jason crazy?

JASON [*overhearing*]:
                                        What do you have to say,
Meleager? Can you say it to my face?

MELEAGER:
How can you risk the lives of so many men of courage and honor
for the sake of a single girl, a foreign woman, a stranger? Are
you out of your mind with lust?

JASON:
                                        Watch yourself, Meleager. This girl—

MELEAGER:
This girl will be the death of us. Look at them! They're all around
    us! It's her
they're after! How could you do this to us?

TIPHYS:
                                        For once, Jason, I agree with him.
Give the girl back. They'll go home and leave us in peace.
No one can deny the Fleece is your right. But her?

[MEDEA *stirs and begins to overhear.*]

POLLUX:
Jason, think. Think of us—our families and our homes.

TIPHYS:
Are you willing to sacrifice our lives for her?

JASON:
What do you say, Idmon? What advice?

IDMON:
This girl is no good, Jason, not for us.

JASON [*weakening*]:
But . . . how could we manage it?
How signal to the Colchian fleet . . . ?

MEDEA [*rising up, and for the first time we see the* MEDEA *of the later tales, enraged and cunning*]:
Do the brave Minya discuss me? Do you talk behind my back?
Am I your wife now, Jason, or merely a captive on your ship?
A handmaid, part of your expedition's loot? Remember, Jason,
we've taken our vows, and I trust them. You cannot put me aside.
Your comrades have sworn no oaths to me, and they might
well think to abandon an inconvenient woman, but you have no
such option. But in truth, none of you do. You think my kinsmen
will be content with me? They want the Fleece, the ship, and
all your lives. Are you afraid? You ought to be! It's only because
of me you're still alive! So listen to me now, Jason—I have a plan to
save all of us. And see us all alive in your port at home.

[*Loud drumming. All depart.*]

HERA [*entering*]:
Daughter of Zeus, are you indifferent to the plight of our
Argonauts? They are surrounded. That brother and fiancé
won't give up!

ATHENA:
                        Could you not have imagined
all of this when you determined we should use Love instead
of another stratagem?

HERA:
Don't argue with me now! We're calling on Boreas
to release his winds.

[*A length of rope drops from the sky.* HERA *catches the end of it. The
wind begins to rise.*]

ATHENA:
Oh no!

HERA:
And direct them to the Colchian fleet.

ATHENA:
But they can't be contained!

HERA:
We'll see about that. We'll make those Colchian
ships bob like corks!

[STYRUS *descends partway down the rope.* HERA *swings it wildly.* STYRUS *can barely hold on, clinging to his own ship's rigging and calling through the storm to the* ARGONAUTS. APSYRTOS *enters, crawling along the deck.*]

STYRUS:
Jason! This is Styrus of Colchis who addresses you!
That woman is mine! Betrothed!

APSYRTOS:
Styrus, he can't hear you! Come down from the rigging! It's getting worse!

STYRUS:
Does she think Jason's better? I could have yoked
those bulls myself and defeated those warriors
without any of her voodoo.

APSYRTOS:
Come down!

STYRUS:
I'll cut off his goddamn head and throw it in the water like bait for fish!

APSYRTOS:
Styrus!

STYRUS:
I'll cut off his goddamn dick and make a eunuch of him!

APSYRTOS:
Now! You'll go under!

STYRUS:
Did Medea conjure this storm with her duppy-dust and her spells?
Is she saving Jason's bacon with her mumbo jumbo again?

APSYRTOS:
Come down!

[STYRUS, *who has been gradually sliding down the rope, now disappears below the deck through the trap.*]

ATHENA:
Too late. He goes under once, twice, three times
and is gone. All the ships are driven to shore.

[ATHENA *pulls all the little boats into a broken heap. A* COLCHIAN
MESSENGER *approaches the grieving* APSYRTOS.]

COLCHIAN MESSENGER:
Apsyrtos, an emissary has come from the Argonauts,
your sister has sent secret word: she wants to come home.
She'll bring you the Fleece tonight on the shores of
the riverbank, near the Argo camp. But you must come
alone. She is so afraid of those barbarians, you cannot
risk a greater force.

[MEDEA *enters with the Fleece around her shoulders. She leans
against the mast in mock distress. As she and her brother speak,*
JASON *silently approaches from behind* APSYRTOS, *his spear drawn.*]

MEDEA:
Oh Brother, how glad I am to see you. If only you
knew what I have been through . . .

APSYRTOS [*accusing*]:
Styrus is dead! Drowned!

MEDEA:
Oh alas!

[*She sinks to the ground.* APSYRTOS *stands above her, threatening.*]

APSYRTOS:
Were those your storms?

MEDEA:
Oh Brother, no! Believe me! I have done nothing but weep since my
capture!

APSYRTOS:
You have the Fleece?

MEDEA:
Yes, here it is. Oh take it from my hands—it
has been the cause of so much suffering.

APSYRTOS:
Let me see it!

[APSYRTOS *grabs at the Fleece just as* JASON *attacks him from behind.* JASON *crushes* APSYRTOS*'s neck against the mast with the shaft
of his spear.* MEDEA *scrambles out from between her brother's legs.*
APSYRTOS *dies. Both* JASON *and* MEDEA *are overcome by what
they've done.*]

MEDEA:
Oh, how will I ever be forgiven?

JASON [*sickened*]:
Let's go.

MEDEA:
Jason?

JASON:
Yes?

MEDEA:
We are bound together forever now. This . . . act. It has bound us.
Forever.

JASON [*after a pause*]:
Yes. I know.

RETURN

[*All the* ARGONAUTS *and* MEDEA *enter. They use their oars like poles,
pushing down into the shallow water.*]

ATHENA:
A storm drove them nine days, and the flood tide carried them
far, far within the Syrtes from which no vessel can return.
Everywhere there are shoals that stretch far into the haze
in all directions. The keel was barely touching water.

POLLUX:
Where are we?

UNCLE:
There's not a living thing!

[*They all throw down their oars.*]

MELEAGER:
                            We should have braved
those rocks again and died on the sea like men
rather than perish here in the desert like rats!

TIPHYS [*breaking down*]:
We're ruined, men. There's no hope of getting seaborne now.
Yet without the flood tide that carried us and now
abandoned us in this desolate place,
we would have broken up miserably at sea,
I assure you!

JASON:
It's true, Tiphys, all of us know you are not to blame.
After all our toil, Zeus does not want us home.

[*The* ARGONAUTS *despair. Music.*]

ATHENA:
Evening's shadows descended. They embraced each other,
said farewell, before each went his separate way
to lie down in the sand and wait to die.

[*Two* GODDESSES OF THE DESERT *appear carrying lanterns. They
kneel down by* JASON *and speak simultaneously.*]

GODDESSES OF THE DESERT:
Jason, rouse yourself.

JASON:
Who are you?

GODDESSES OF THE DESERT:
We are the guardians of the desert, Jason. We know
the whole tally of your ordeals. Rise up, be brave,
gather your crew, and offer full recompense
to the mother who bore you so long in her belly.
Move straight ahead and you will reach the sea.

[*The* GODDESSES OF THE DESERT *disappear. Music ends.*]

ATHENA:
The Libyan sun was roasting them.

JASON:
Idmon! Crew! Gather round. Just now—just now
two women came to me—goddesses, I think, and said
we should arise and give "full recompense" to our mother
for all the long pains she suffered as she carried us
in her belly and we would reach the sea. What can it mean?

[ATHENA *embraces* IDMON *from behind, her hand on his heart.*]

IDMON:
Friends, our mother, I'd guess, is none else than our ship;
it's true she has us forever in her belly and groans
at the troublesome labors we set her to. I believe,
my friends, we are to recompense her by carrying
her straight into the desert where we may find
some inlet to the sea.

[*During the following, the* ARGONAUTS *take up their oars and place them across their shoulders.* MEDEA *rides on* JASON'*s shoulders. They struggle step-by-step, bent double under the weight of the ship.*]

ALL:
This story belongs to the Muses, I sing in obedience;
and the tale I heard as true was that you, O brave seamen,
through your strength, your endurance, did over the desert dunes
of Libya bear your vessel, and all the gear she carried,
high on your shoulders, for a dozen days and nights on end.

[*The* ARGONAUTS *collapse.*]

ATHENA:
They found the sea all right, but on the morning they
arose to set sail once more—

[*All the* ARGONAUTS *are leaving. But* IDMON *doesn't move, apparently asleep on the ground.*]

JASON:
Idmon? How can you want to sleep when at last—
Idmon? [*Approaching him*] Idmon?

ATHENA:
It was a fever that took him. Nothing more.

HERA:
He was the first to go.

[JASON *plants* IDMON'*s oar upright, through the grating on the deck.*]

ATHENA:
Yes, then Tiphys right after.

[TIPHYS *plants his own oar and lies down beside it.*]

HERA:
Snake bite.

[*All the living* ARGONAUTS *have left except* MELEAGER *and* UNCLE.]

ATHENA:
Then Meleager, and his uncle. Most trivial of all.

UNCLE:
Fetch the water, Nephew.

MELEAGER:
What do you mean? I did it yesterday.

UNCLE:
And I did it for three days before that.

MELEAGER:
It's not my turn.

UNCLE:
It is your turn.

MELEAGER:
No one asked you to do it three days in a row. Fetch it yourself, Uncle.

UNCLE:
It's your turn.

MELEAGER:
It is not my turn.

UNCLE:
Why won't you ever—?

MELEAGER [*just going insane*]:
No! You get it! You get it! You get it!

[MELEAGER *repeatedly stabs* UNCLE, *who dies.* MELEAGER'S MOTHER *enters, carrying a half-burnt log.* MELEAGER *watches her in sorrow.*]

HERA:
I heard when Meleager's mother heard, she
went to the casket where she kept that half-burnt log,
the one that she had snatched from the fire the day
he was born when the gods declared his life would
last only as long as that piece of wood.

MELEAGER'S MOTHER:
Burn, child, burn as you should have done long ago.
I loved my brother more than you.

[*She lets the log roll into the fire (the trap).* MELEAGER, *watching her, dies. During the following, all* ARGONAUTS *enter and are resurrected and each takes up his old rowing place along the edges of the deck.* MEDEA *and* JASON *enter from opposite sides and stand facing each other.* MEDEA *is draped in the Fleece. As they speak,* JASON *is slowly backing away.*]

ATHENA:

The *Argo* staggered home. Glory. Rejoicing. Pelias
already dead. Jason's parents and little brother dead.
And the inevitable.

JASON:

                                          I ask you to understand. You
must understand. I'm in a position now . . . If I marry her
I will regain the throne. The throne of Thessaly itself.

MEDEA:

I had a kingdom once. But I gave it up. Here
are my vast realms: the square foot where I stand.

JASON:

It's not—it's not about you. Don't you see? And you
have the children now, our two children! They will
be your home—all the home you need.

MEDEA:

                                          Do you love her?

JASON:

It's not— I— It's not about how I treat you or you
treat me. It's all—it's so much larger.

[*He exits. The door closes behind him.*]

MEDEA:

                                          I see.

[*During the following,* MEDEA *drops the Golden Fleece and takes off the little harness that has held the arrow to her chest. She lets it fall to the floor and exits with* ATHENA *and* HERA *following.*]

ARGONAUTS:
Oh these glorious missions of men, they start out so well,
so full of hope and noble intent: teach the foreigner a lesson,
destroy the tyrant, become a man, defend the nation,
hip, hip, hoorah, hoorah. Seize that shining Fleece
and the world itself will change, seize that Golden Fleece
and utopia will descend, seize that Fleece and
there will be an end to evil.

        Whatever.

They all end up like this in the end.

[*All the* ARGONAUTS *exit.*]

CONCLUSION

[ATHENA *and* HERA *enter.* HERA *is carrying a bucket, a wedding veil, and a white dress over her arm.* ATHENA *is dragging a dirty, old sailcloth wrapped around something heavy.*]

ATHENA:
Where shall we put her?

HERA:
Doesn't matter. With the rest of the discards.

ATHENA:
She served us pretty well.

[*She is unfolding the cloth.* MEDEA *is crumpled up inside.*]

HERA:
Well, she didn't have a choice.

ATHENA:
Poor thing.

HERA:
What do you mean? You know what she did—what she went on
to do.

ATHENA:
I know.

[ATHENA *rouses* MEDEA, *who sits up, dazed.*]

HERA:
Killed the girl he was to marry—setting her on fire, slaughtered the
two little boys.

ATHENA:
I know, I know.

HERA:
How can you ask them to have pity for her? A woman who killed
her own children.

[MEDEA *goes to the bucket, kneels down, and strips off her bloody
dress. She washes it in the bucket.*]

ATHENA:

But . . . Don't think of the children in the story as actual children. Think of them instead as her own heart, her own broken heart; and the murder as the willful destruction of her own ability to love. They do that, you know, when they've had enough. Or think of the children they had together as the return of those two who flew away on the golden ram, the beginning of it all, saved miraculously—but unnaturally—from death by one mother to finally meet their true fate through another.

[MEDEA *wrings the water out of her bloody dress over the bucket then drops the dress in.*]

HERA:

It's a stretch.

ATHENA:

But why else would it end the way it does—with grace?

HERA:

I know.

ATHENA:

Help me here. Help me help her change.

[*They approach* MEDEA, *who passively raises her arms for the new white dress, identical to her first dress.* HERA *and* ATHENA *drop it over her arms and fuss a little, fixing it.*]

HERA [*quietly, a little embarrassed*]:

This dress has a zipper.

ATHENA:
I know.

HERA [*again embarrassed*]:
Not very authentic.

ATHENA:
No. But then . . . a sheep that flies? And a dragon who doesn't sleep and all the rest? Don't be so literal. You miss a lot.

[*They get the dress zipped up.* MEDEA *stands.*]

HERA:
There. She's done.

ATHENA:
Not quite.

HERA:
No. Not quite. Funny how no one talks about it much.

[HERA *takes up the wedding veil and puts it on* MEDEA's *head and fusses with it a little. Throughout this,* MEDEA *is passive.*]

ATHENA:
The second marriage?

[MEDEA *peers out as though gazing into a mirror. She smiles.*]

HERA:
Yes. The happy one. To Achilles's ghost in the underworld.

[ATHENA *leads* MEDEA *to the trapdoor.* MEDEA *starts to descend.*]

ATHENA:
Yes, she is a queen there, she never dies. Her realms are the Elysian fields.

[*She closes the trapdoor behind* MEDEA. JASON *enters. He is very old and still wearing only one sandal. He limps along slowly. His hair is gray, and he wears rags.*]

HERA:
And what of him? The man for whom Love was not enough?

ATHENA:
After it all happened, after the death of his new young bride, the new young princess for whom he abandoned little Medea, after her death and those of his children at Medea's hand, he was considered cursed. An ill-omened man. He became an exile. Wandered for years alone. One day he came to an abandoned cove, a bleak corner of the sea, cold and ugly and unloved, full of rocky edges and eelgrass and foam, and he saw there on the beach a pile of rotting wood, a wreck.

JASON [*touching the mast*]:
The *Argo*?

ATHENA:
The *Argo*. The remains of her. Bleached out by the sun, rotten and crawling with insects, only the mast still recognizable, leaning against the broken hull. He thought:

JASON:
Enough's enough.

145

[*He takes the edge of the old sailcloth and starts to twist it.*]

ATHENA:
Found the old hawser. Gray and chewed up by the sea, but still strong enough. And he thought that he might hang himself by the mast.

HERA:
We mustn't let that happen.

ATHENA:
No: we'll let the wreck fall on him and crush him into the sand.

[JASON *collapses. Pause.*]

HERA:
Not a glorious end.

ATHENA:
No.

[*Pause.*]

HERA:
What happened to the rest? Where are they?

ATHENA:
Look up.

[*Music.*]

There in the sky, the zodiacal signs
that journey forever. All of them are there.

146

[*One by one each character enters, takes up a different position on-stage, and slowly turns. As each speaks, little lights, little patterns of constellations illuminate on him or her. The stage darkens.*]

TIPHYS [*carrying the golden ram*]:
Aries, the ram, is Phrixus's ram, the one that started the whole thing.

UNCLE:
And Taurus, the bull, is Aeëtes's, the fire-breathing one.

MELEAGER:
The scales of Libra are those Meleager's mother
used to weigh her love for her brother and her son.

IDMON:
The goat is the symbol of the lusty doings at Lemnos.

HYLAS:
Hylas makes Aquarius, holding the pitcher of water.

CASTOR AND POLLUX:
The twins of Gemini are Castor and Pollux, of course.

HERCULES:
And the archer is Hercules, still firing at the sun and waves.

JASON:
The fish, Pisces, in one version is said to have swallowed
Jason and spat him up again.

ATALANTA AND ANDROMEDA:
The serpent is Scorpio, who guarded the Fleece.

ATHENA:
Which leaves us only Virgo, the maiden princess Medea herself.

[MEDEA *appears in the sky, little lights around her body. She slowly spins.*]

Look up: every night you see them, wherever you are,
even in the cities, in New York or Bangkok, in Cairo or Chicago—
sailing, still sailing, even as we sleep.

[*All the constellations fade. Music ends.*]

A NOTE ON THE CASTING

The original production of *Argonautika* had a cast of fourteen (five women and nine men), but the show would be much more easily accomplished and perhaps benefit in other ways from a larger cast. With fourteen, the number of Argonauts on stage at any given time varies greatly; and although there are four women of Lemnos, only three may appear on stage at the same time. The original division of roles is listed below, but many of these tracks (particularly those of the Second through Seventh Man), could be divided up differently according to the strengths of your own cast.

FIRST WOMAN: Hera, Alcimede, Third Woman of Lemnos

SECOND WOMAN: Athena

THIRD WOMAN: Medea, Rumor, Dryope, Second Woman of Lemnos

FOURTH WOMAN: Andromeda, Pelias's Son, Fourth Woman of Lemnos, Eros, Goddess of the Desert

FIFTH WOMAN: Aphrodite, Atalanta, First Woman of Lemnos, Goddess of the Desert, Meleager's Mother

FIRST MAN: Jason

SECOND MAN: Idmon, Cepheus

THIRD MAN: Meleager, Asterion, Boreas, Zetes, Euphemos

FOURTH MAN: Pelias, Tiphys

FIFTH MAN: Castor, Ghost, Phineus, Fury, Apsyrtos

SIXTH MAN: Pollux

SEVENTH MAN: Uncle, Polyphemus, Amycus, Styrus

EIGHTH MAN: Hercules, Aeëtes

NINTH MAN: Hylas, Dymas

APPENDIX: ADDITIONAL NOTES
ON THE STAGING OF *ARGONAUTIKA*

Because I only write my scripts concurrent with the process of rehearsal and not in advance, and because I am always present to directly communicate or develop with the performers all of the movement and staging of the story, the original performance text, brought into the room bit by bit, day by day, contains no stage directions whatsoever. Yet, because the texts I adapt were not originally intended for the stage, they often contain many impossible creatures, landscapes, and occurrences for which real-life stage solutions must be found. Long after the production, when it comes time to publish, I am never sure how much description of the staging to include in the body of the script. Should I make a script for the reader who wishes to enter fully into the imaginative world of the story (where a sea monster is just a sea monster)? Or for someone seriously thinking of staging the show (where how the sea monster might actually manifest on stage is described)?

I have not wanted to dictate how a particular fantastical or epic occurrence should transpire in new productions of my plays because I think there are many ways to be perfect, and because finding one's own solutions to storytelling problems is one of the primary joys of directing. At the same time, I understand that the original way these images were accomplished created meanings, feelings, and a particular aesthetic that was fundamental to the experience of the show. Because I direct these adaptations as I write them, the spoken text is even more than usually dependent on the physical image of the moment; indeed, the text is often shaped by the image rather than the other way around. I am always afraid that in the absence of the image the text may seem incomplete, quirky, or rhythmically odd. I have also discovered that many potential directors are quite eager to understand how things were originally accomplished. In seeking to accommodate both sorts of readers and directors, as well as my own concerns, I have settled on keeping the mechanics of the original stage image within the body of the script to a minimum, but adding an appendix, such as this, where these mechanics are further explained. In every instance, many other creative solutions are possible.

THE SEA MONSTER IN "ANDROMEDA"

During the early part of the "Andromeda" scene, a large piece of green fabric was stretched across the stage and moved by performers in such a way as to suggest the roiling of the sea. The monster was created when an actor arose from the trap below the material and another performer placed into his (hidden) hands two eyeballs. The actor moved about the stage as a sea monster until his destruction, at which point his eyeballs popped out into the air and he sank back into the trap, pulling the whole of the cloth (the sea, his body) down behind him. The performers holding the periphery of the cloth had to practice to keep it in motion and yet hide the body of the monster-actor as he moved around.

AMYCUS

The ferocious boxer Amycus was created by one actor sitting on another's shoulders, wearing an enormous head and holding two extended, gloved hands. Both actors were covered by the same long robe. The lower actor manipulated the large, snaggle-toothed mouth of the puppet head with strings while the upper actor was in charge of the arms. When Amycus is killed, both actors fell to the ground, separated, and walked offstage defeated, dragging the head and arms.

THE HARPIES

The Harpies were our most technically sophisticated puppets. They were large, shabby, winged creatures on long poles with controls that allowed one of them to defecate (wet rags) and another to vomit (more wet rags) onto Phineus. They could easily be embodied by actors.

THE BABY (JASON'S LITTLE BROTHER)

The baby was a simple marionette, soft, fairly featureless, and yet the best puppet of all. He was lowered through the opening in the ceiling of the set into Alcimede's arms and controlled by a crew member above. His strings were attached to his arms, legs, and head. It is important that he move continuously but only very slightly throughout the scene until his terrible death, when his strings are cut.

BIRDS, THE CENTAUR, AND OTHER CREATURES

There were a number of bird puppets—single birds and arrangements of birds on long poles—some of whose wings could be controlled by wires and levers. There was a centaur created by an actor who wore a skeletal horse's back protruding from his waist. He wore large, black, high-heeled shoes. The actor's ankles were rigged to the back legs of the horse, so that all four legs of the centaur could move. The dragon that guards the Golden Fleece was a single, illuminated large eyeball, supported by a brace around the performer's waist, with a lid that could droop and close. The bulls that Jason battles were no more than two performers with horns on their heads and tails around their waists, accompanied by a great deal of smoke. The skeleton soldiers were a variety of small and larger Halloween skeletons manipulated by several actors.

THE GOLDEN RAM AND PHRIXUS AND HELLE

In the "Pelias Was Old" scene, one performer had a little box containing two figurines—the children Phrixus and Helle—as well as some white powder, and a second performer carried the golden ram. Throughout Pelias's narration of the tale, each incident was lightly illustrated. The first performer revealed the figurines as they were named, let fall some powder from his hand to illustrate the death of the crops, blew a bit of it from his palm when the golden ram lands, raising "a little cloud of dust," and so forth. The ram was fairly small, winged, and golden and was mounted on a tall detachable pole. It had two pegs on its back on which the children could be fastened. As it flew, the performer pulled one of those pegs down by means of rigging threaded through the Fleece and the pole, causing Helle to fall "into the sea" (caught by the other performer). This was a very elaborate mechanical puppet; something much simpler could serve just as well. The story need not be illustrated at all, but doing so introduces the physical ram to the stage, where he remains throughout the first act, his golden coat shining above all the action. When Jason retrieves the Fleece in the second act, it was merely a piece of gold fabric.

FLYING

Flying was accomplished in many ways. Eros was indeed on wires that lowered him and raised him through the opening in the ceiling of the set. Other flying was just "pretend," with extended arms and raised legs. The primary method of flying, however, was lifts: Hera was lifted by several performers and whisked away for her first exit, and Athena was often floating in the air, held at the hips by a single extremely strong and able performer.

MUSIC AND SOUND DESIGN

Amycus, the Ghost, and Boreas were amplified so that some distortion could be used on their voices. Athena and Hera were not generally amplified for effect, but often were for audibility's sake when they were speaking narration over underscoring. Any sizable passage of narration should be underscored if only by something atmospheric. Music drives the transitions and shifts the mood and rhythm of the show. I encourage original music in all productions, but if you care to license what is available from Andre Pluess, contact him through his website at pluess-sussman.red-bean.com.

MODIFICATIONS TO THE TEXT IN PRODUCTION

If all is going well, the show should not feel overlong. However, if circumstances demand a shorter show, you could excise the entire "Visitation" scene in the first act. Move straight from "Launch" to "Boreas" and trim Athena's first line there. This move would probably imply, but not require, losing the second half of the "Hallway" scene where Pelias's son is introduced and losing that character altogether. While "Visitation" contains many theatrical delights, it does take the audience back to shore just as the *Argo* has launched, and it doesn't truly push the plot forward. It is a very Roman scene, drawn from the Flaccus version of the tale.

If you are lucky enough to have a large cast, you can give some of the Argonauts a more consistent presence (Zetes, for instance) and make up a verse for them to introduce themselves during "Roll Call" (it is also fun to use the Roll Call to introduce each of the cast by name during the curtain call). Due to the spare cast size of the first production, Pelias's son never had much presence once the *Argo* had launched (the actor had to play so many other parts) and I always felt this was a shame. If you have more actors, feel free to keep Pelias's son around, assigning this or that spare line to him. Just be sure to kill him off before the return. He could die alongside Tiphys and Idmon by some sad, innocent means such as having run off in pursuit of a rabbit and never returning.

Finally, in the last line of the play, you should substitute the name of your own city or town for "Chicago."

Jason (Ryan Artzberger)

Castor (Larry DiStasi) and Pollux (Tony Hernandez) at the Roll Call

The Launch

The *Argo* sails away, abandoning Hercules.

The Argonauts confront Amycus the Boxer (David Catlin).

Hera (Lisa Tejero) and Athena (Mariann Mayberry) conspire to help Jason.

Aphrodite (Angela Walsh) instructs Eros (Victoria Caciopoli, airborne) to shoot Medea with one of his arrows.

The Argonauts mired in the shoals

ABOUT THE DIRECTOR AND PLAYWRIGHT

Mary Zimmerman's credits as an adapter and a director include *Metamorphoses, The Arabian Nights, The Odyssey, Journey to the West, Eleven Rooms of Proust, Silk, The Secret in the Wings, Mirror of the Invisible World, The White Snake,* and *The Notebooks of Leonardo da Vinci.* Her work has been produced at the Lookingglass Theatre and Goodman Theatre of Chicago; on Broadway at Circle in the Square; in New York at Second Stage, the Brooklyn Academy of Music, and the Manhattan Theatre Club; at the Mark Taper Forum in Los Angeles; and at the McCarter, Berkeley Repertory, and Seattle Repertory as well as many other theaters around the country and abroad. She has also directed at the Metropolitan Opera. Zimmerman is the recipient of a MacArthur Fellowship and won a Tony Award for her direction of *Metamorphoses.* She is a professor of performance studies at Northwestern University.